BETTER BIBLE TEACHING

for JUNIORS

IN THE SUNDAY SCHOOL

by

LILLIAN MOORE RICE

CONVENTION PRESS
Nashville, Tennessee

Copyright, 1952

BROADMAN PRESS

Nashville, Tennessee

5117-53

Code Number: Church Study Course

This book is number 1753 in category 17, section for
Adults and Young People.

Library of Congress Catalog Card Number: 52-13859

Printed in the United States of America

7.5 AL 66 R.R.D.

To a Good Teacher

My Mother

Susan Ansley Moore

ABOUT THE AUTHOR

OF HER background experience in Junior work, Mrs. Rice says, "I began teaching Juniors when I was little more than an Intermediate (much too young for such a responsible task, of course), and I have spent all the years since working with that age exclusively.

"Ours was a one-room church building in those days, and my first class met in the little dark rectangle between pulpit and baptistry. We lacked everything in the way of material equipment, maps, pictures, tables, chalkboard—all the teaching aids that today we know are right and good. I learned early and I learned through hard experience the importance of using activities in guiding the learning of Juniors, and the teacher's need for guidance in using activities.

"As I grew up, so did our Sunday school. Soon we were departmentized, in a new building, and I was the Junior superintendent. The responsibility for finding, enlisting, and training teachers brought some experiences that I thought might be shared with others, so I wrote a few articles for *The Junior Teacher*. Soon I was asked to write Sunday school lessons for Juniors, Uniform Lessons first, then Graded Lessons. For seventeen years I was superintendent of Junior work for the Baptist Sunday School Board. In 1961 I became children's book editor for Broadman Press."

Mrs. Rice grew up and lived most of her life in Decatur, Georgia. She attended Agnes Scott College, Oglethorpe University, and studied creative writing and journalism at the University of Georgia Extension School. Since coming to Nashville, she has studied at Peabody College in the field of elementary education.

CONTENTS

CHURCH STUDY COURSE

THE CHURCH STUDY COURSE began October 1, 1959. It is a merger of three courses previously promoted by the Sunday School Board—the Sunday School Training Course, the Graded Training Union Study Course, and the Church Music Training Course. On October 1, 1961, the Woman's Missionary Union principles and methods studies were added.

The course is fully graded. The system of awards provides a series of five diplomas of twenty books each for Adults or Young People, two diplomas of five books each for Intermediates, and two diplomas of five books each for Juniors.

The course is comprehensive, with books grouped into twenty categories. The purpose of the course is to help Christians to grow in knowledge and conviction, to help them to grow toward maturity in Christian character and competence for service, to encourage them to participate worthily as workers in their churches, and to develop leaders for all phases of church life and work.

The Church Study Course is promoted by the Baptist Sunday School Board, 127 Ninth Avenue, North, Nashville, Tennessee 37203, through its Sunday School, Training Union, Church Music, and Church Administration departments; by the Woman's Missionary Union, 600 North Twentieth Street, Birmingham, Alabama 35203; and by the respective departments in the states affiliated with the Southern Baptist Convention. A description of the course and the system of awards may be found in the leaflet "Trained Workmen," which may be obtained without charge from any one of these departments.

A record of all awards earned should be maintained in each church. A person should be designated by the church to keep the files. Forms for such records may be ordered from any Baptist Book Store.

REQUIREMENTS FOR CREDIT IN CLASS OR HOME STUDY

IF CREDIT IS DESIRED for the study of this book in a class or by home study, the following requirements must be met:

I. IN CLASSWORK

1. The class must meet a minimum of seven and one-half clock hours. The required time does not include assembly periods. Ten class periods of forty-five minutes each are recommended. (If laboratory or clinical work is desired in specialized or technical courses, this requirement may be met by six clock hours of classwork and three clock hours of supervised laboratory or clinical work).

2. A class member who attends all class sessions and completes the reading of the book within a week following the last class session will not be required to do any written work for credit.

3. A class member who is absent from one or more sessions must answer the questions (pp. 151-152) on all chapters he misses. In such a case, he must turn in his paper within a week, and he must certify that he has read the book.

4. The teacher should request an award for himself. A person who teaches a book in the section for Intermediates or Juniors (any category) or conducts an approved unit of instruction for Nursery, Beginner, or Primary children will be granted an award in category 11, Special Studies, which will count as an elective on his own diploma. He should specify in his request the name of the book taught, or the unit conducted for Nursery, Beginner, or Primary children.

5. The teacher should complete the "Request for Book Awards—Class Study" (Form 150) and forward it within

REQUIREMENTS FOR CREDIT

two weeks after the completion of the class to the Church Study Course Awards Office, 127 Ninth Avenue, North, Nashville, Tennessee 37203.

II. IN HOME STUDY

1. A person who does not attend any class session may receive credit by answering all questions for written work as indicated in the book (pp. 151-152). When a person turns in his paper on home study, he must certify that he has read the book.

2. Students may find profit in studying the text together, but individual papers are required. Carbon copies or duplicates in any form cannot be accepted.

3. Home study work papers may be graded by the pastor or a person designated by him, or they may be sent to the Church Study Course Awards Office for grading. The form entitled "Request for Book Awards—Home Study" (Form 151) must be used in requesting awards. It should be mailed to Church Study Course Awards Office, 127 Ninth Avenue, North, Nashville, Tennessee 37203.

III. CREDIT FOR THIS BOOK

This book is number 1753 in category 17, section for Adults and Young People.

I
JUNIORS AND

It is easy to get a Junior to lieve in Jesus—*but he must belie*

CHAPTER I

JUNIORS AND JESUS

And when he was twelve years old, . . . they found him in the temple, sitting in the midst of the doctors, both hearing them, and asking them questions.

And all that heard him were astonished at his understanding and answers. . . .

And he said unto them, How is it that ye sought me? wist ye not that I must be about my Father's business?

And he went down with them, and came to Nazareth and was subject unto them . . .

And Jesus increased in wisdom and stature, and in favour with God and man. (From Luke 2:42-52)

This is a book about Juniors and how to guide them in the Sunday school. It is written to help the men and women who work with them on Sunday morning understand a little more clearly how Juniors think and feel and learn and grow. It is written in the hope that they may use that understanding to help their boys and girls know and love Jesus, become his followers, then grow in ways that will honor him and serve his work.

I. STUDYING JESUS AT TWELVE

So we start this book about Juniors with the story of a twelve-year-old. In all the world we could find no words so right for introducing our subject. Jesus did many things during his boyhood—we know that—but the Bible tells us only one thing. He said many things during the years when he was growing up in Nazareth, the "silent years," we call them, but the Bible tells us only one thing: something he did and something he said when he was twelve, a Junior.

[3]

For Junior workers the story of Jesus at twelve holds special interest and significance. Our relationship to a little group of boys or girls sharpens our interest in the Juniorhood of Jesus. What was he like as a Boy? What were the things he enjoyed doing? What were his special interests? We read the story with our Junior eyes, searching every detail in an effort to bring our own picture of the twelve-year-old Jesus into clearer focus. We read it with the eyes of teachers, wondering if we can find in the example of Jesus as a Junior some suggestions for guiding our own Juniors, some purposes to work toward in our teaching.

And we find that:

Jesus loved his Father's house, and found in his worship and study there the highest satisfactions for his mind and spirit.

Every line of this passage confirms that truth. His words to Mary, "How was it that ye sought me?" imply surprise at her lack of understanding. It was as if he had said, "How could you have looked for me anywhere else but here?" The American Standard Version translates his next question, "Knew ye not that I must be in my Father's house?" He *must.* But the "must" was from within, not from without. The compulsion was love and interest, the desire to nourish mind and spirit, to honor and please God, the need for that special closeness to God that comes from meeting the Father in his own house.

Jesus was interested in the study of God's Word. So many fascinating things were going on in this wonderful Temple, so much that a twelve-year-old would want to explore and observe. But for the Boy from Nazareth one group exerted the greatest fascination of all: a group engaged in the study of the Scriptures; a group of teachers and their pupils, we would say. ("Teachers," authorities tell us, is the real meaning of the word "doctors.") These learned men were not preaching. They were not lecturing merely—or exhorting. They were explaining. They were asking questions. They were encouraging questions from the group. They were *teaching*. They were helping the people who came to the house of worship to get a better understanding of God's Word.

Jesus took part in the study and discussion of God's Word. When Jesus joined the group around the wise men, he brought so much more than his physical body. He brought a wide-awake mind, an eager interest in every aspect of the subjects being discussed. He contributed. He shared. The Bible tells us he listened to the teachers. But he was not a hearer only. He asked questions and answered them. He used his mind. He thought. He concentrated.

Jesus honored God by doing his will, not only in the house of worship, but in his home and all other places.

Into the wonderfully stimulating environment of the Temple came Mary and Joseph bringing to an end the lovely adventure. He must go home now, back to the little rural village where there were no wise scholars, no beautiful temple, no heart-stirring opportunities like those in Jerusalem.

But Jesus "went down with them, and came to Nazareth."

It is at this point that the Bible tells us a beautiful thing, just one more small detail, but one that lights up another aspect of the character of Jesus: "And he was subject unto them." The Boy whose mentality and understanding had astonished the wisest scholars in Israel submitted to the authority of the two humble people in the little Nazareth home. Jesus obeyed Joseph and Mary. He respected their wishes, deferred to their will. And we know that the Nazareth household was happier, its atmosphere sweeter and more harmonious because of the spirit and influence of the twelve-year-old Jesus.

Jesus grew—grew in mind and body and spirit, grew in closeness to God and in love and understanding of those around him. He grew whole and complete and all-around, inner growth keeping pace always with physical growth.

It is a beautiful picture for Junior workers to study, this picture of Jesus at twelve. It is one we should contemplate reverently, devotionally, not only as a spiritual exercise, but as a guide for our own work as teachers. So many of the areas in which workers need to help their boys and girls are suggested here—the areas of church attendance, Bible study, home relations. That is one reason for beginning this book with the Boy Jesus.

But there is another reason. By putting Jesus at the very beginning, I have tried to say that we put him first in our work with Juniors, that all we do for boys and girls in these important Junior years relates in some way to him, to the things he taught and lived and stood for and died for—the things he wants to see lived out by those who love him today.

II. INTRODUCING JUNIORS TO JESUS

It is absolutely essential that Jesus have central place in our work with boys and girls nine, ten, eleven, and twelve years of age. The needs of this age group demand that the teaching about Jesus take on a new emphasis now, a deeper meaning. Up until now the child has been hearing of Jesus as his Friend, One who loves him, One whom the Father sent to be the Saviour of the world. But now with developing conscience and maturing mind, he is ready for a more personal understanding of Jesus, ready to be led into an experience of trust in Jesus, ready to recognize him not only as "*the*" Saviour, but as "*my*" Saviour.

In Junior years one purpose has first claim on our hearts and efforts: *to lead boys and girls to trust Jesus as Saviour and Lord of their lives*. That is the Junior worker's highest opportunity and greatest challenge.

That is not to say that we should minimize the importance of character training, of helping Juniors build into their lives those great Christian principles of integrity, honor, purity, love, compassion, and concern for others. It means we are seeking to provide a way through which those great ideals may be developed and strengthened in a Junior's life, the way of Christian discipleship.

To try to help a child of Junior age grow a fine Christian character without helping him first to root that growth in something permanent and enduring, in soil that is deep and rich and capable of nourishing growth—that is to put *second* things first. A rootless life is a fruitless life.

Faith in Jesus is the only enduring foundation on which to build sound Christian character.

1. *Juniors Are Ready for the Experience of Faith*

The experience of the years confirms the fact that Juniors are ready to be led into an experience of trust and faith in Jesus. Juniors are old enough to realize something of what it means that God so loved *them*— a Junior boy, a Junior girl—that he sent his Son; old enough to respond to that love with an answering love.

It is this love of God's that we should magnify in leading Juniors into an experience of conversion. They should turn to Jesus in a glad and voluntary act of surrender, impelled not by fear or guilt, but by a love in whose light their own wrongness before God is revealed, a love that makes it imperative that they be right before God.

Juniors are old enough to know that wrongdoing is sin, and to realize that the wrong things they feel and do right now—hate and anger, disobedience, jealousy and selfishness—are sins, the result of the roots of sin in every heart that cripple a life and hurt a soul. Juniors are old enough to grasp the truth that no person in the world can cure his own soul of the disease called sin; that not even mother or father can do that, or teacher or preacher—that only Jesus can do something about the root of sin in a heart.

Juniors are old enough for all these experiences. They are close enough to adulthood to have the necessary mental maturity, but they are also close enough to childhood to have the capacity for trust and simplicity of faith that are conditions for entering the kingdom. Juniors have not reached the age of doubt; these are the years when, as someone has said, "there are no shadows in the thinking."

2. *We Should Win Juniors While They Are Juniors*

We were in the midst of a revival in my church, and on a particular night only one person came forward in response to the invitation: a nine-year-old boy. My preacher asked the boy to turn around to face the congregation. He put his arm across his shoulders. He said to the people facing him, "Sometimes we act as if the supreme result of an evangelistic service is the winning of adults. But"—and his voice became very thoughtful—"I wonder whether that standard is Jesus' standard." Then he added, "There is nothing in the world more valuable than a saved soul except—a saved soul *plus* a saved life."

(1) *Juniors have most of life before them.*—That statement suggests a primary reason for winning Juniors while they are Juniors. They have most of life before them rather than behind them. They have the good

years, the young, virile, productive years, not just the years of inactivity and decline.

"How many were converted tonight?" a friend asked Dwight L. Moody.

"Two and a half," replied the evangelist.

"You mean two adults and a child?"

"No, two children and an adult. The man had only half a life to give the Lord."

(2) *Those coming early into the church make the best leaders.*—Many, many times, in addressing groups of Sunday school leaders I have asked, "How old were you when you made your decision for Christ?" And always I have found that in these groups of church workers, Sunday school leaders, the majority of them accepted Christ when they were under fourteen.

Thus I have come to accept the fact that those coming early to Christ and early into the church are those who make the church its best leaders.

(3) *Juniors need Jesus now.*—There is still another reason. Juniors need Jesus right now, need him to save them from sin, and to help them every day while they are nine, ten, eleven, twelve—and all the years beyond. One of the penalties of waiting until later years is that the Junior misses so many years of friendship with Jesus, so many years of the help that even boys and girls desperately need in meeting the testing-times of life.

3. *These Are Requirements for Winning Juniors*

I overheard a conversation between a pastor and a young woman whom he was trying to enlist as a Sunday school teacher. Very reluctant to commit herself, the young woman finally explained the reason: "I know I could teach the lessons," she said. "What I don't know is that I have the special training for—evangelism."

Two errors in that young woman's thinking are apparent. In the first place, she thought that lessons were one thing, and evangelism another thing. They are, of course, two parts of a whole. Evangelism is an end, a goal, and lessons are a means toward that goal. The teacher uses his lessons to achieve his greatest goal—bringing about a meeting between Juniors and Jesus.

In the second place, the young woman thought that winning to Christ is something that requires extraordinary abilities and training, abilities beyond the capacity of a mere layman. Fortunately the wise pastor set her right. "You don't need theological training to help make Christ real to Juniors," he said. "What you need very much is knowledge of three simple, fundamental things—knowledge of your Bible, personal knowledge of Jesus, knowledge of your Juniors."

That is sane and practical counsel for any Sunday school teacher who is serious about his responsibility for helping boys and girls trust Jesus.

(1) *A teacher must know what the Bible teaches about becoming a Christian.*—The best evangelism, the kind that is most effective with Juniors, is based on knowledge of God's Word, and the ability to make that word plain to boys and girls. That is why the Sunday school teacher has an opportunity superior to that of anybody else in winning his pupils to Christ. As he sits with them Sunday after Sunday; as he guides them in searching the Bible, in discussing the meaning of the passages they read, that teacher is laying a foundation for a sound and durable evangelism. He is proceeding in the order called for by Jesus when he said "Go . . . teach . . . baptize" (Matt. 28:19).

Of course this means that a teacher must have not only an understanding of the message of the whole Bible, but a special grasp of those passages that relate to this particular subject. He should be so familiar with certain verses that he can turn to them at any time, or can quote them from memory. Such verses as John 3:16; Luke 19:10; 1 John 4:14; Acts 16:31; Romans 5:8; and Hebrews 7:25 should be required memory work for teachers of Juniors.

(2) *A teacher must know Jesus through personal experience.*—There is a great deal of difference between knowing *about* Jesus and *knowing* Jesus. A teacher who can say, "I know whom I have believed" is a teacher who at some time has undergone a personal experience of conversion—a turning around with Jesus, which is the true meaning of "convert." This means turning away from the old life where conduct was dictated by selfish desire, to a new willingness to let Jesus' will and desire and standards determine life directions—the same sort of surrender that Paul implied when he said, "Lord, what wilt thou have me to do?"

The requirement that a teacher be one who knows from experience what it means to make a personal commitment to Christ is critically important for teachers of boys and girls. A teacher cannot enrich a pupil's understanding of Christ beyond his own; he cannot lead another into a true relationship with Christ unless he himself is rightly related to him.

It is easy to lead Juniors to make a profession of faith, join the church and undergo baptism before they have had the experience of faith which must precede these outward expressions. The teacher whose experience of Christ is real will want that same kind of experience for his pupils; he will pray that the Juniors may have an actual *experience* of Jesus before coming into the church.

(3) *A teacher must know how to put Bible terms into Junior language.*—A teacher must be able to sense the Junior's capacity for understanding the necessity for salvation and for entering into that experience. Many fine Christians fail at this point simply because they do not

know how to translate the terms associated with conversion into terms that Juniors can understand. They try to force the Junior's understanding into an adult mold.

Dr. E. Y. Mullins in his helpful book *Talks on Soul-Winning* offers this practical counsel on this point:

In dealing with children . . . we must avoid the long or the unusual word. We must avoid doctrinal phrases and theological terms. We must state the Christian life in its most elementary principles.

For the child the Christian life is following Jesus, or obeying his commands, or loving the Saviour and serving him. All these and other simple forms of expression containing the same ideas are adapted to convey to the mind of the child the meaning of the Christian life. Turning away from wrongdoing, putting away evil thoughts, giving up all sin, forsaking the things that do harm, are forms of expression conveying clear ideas which are equivalent to repentance.

Love, trust, faith, obedience, service, duty and loyalty are ideas which can be made plain to the child, and it is in such terms as these that our appeal to children must be made.

III. Helping Juniors Grow as Christians

It is tragic when a baby fails to grow after he is born. It is tragic, too, when a Christian fails to grow after he is born again.

As we seek through our lessons, our influence, our living, and through personal talks with our Juniors to help them trust Jesus as Saviour, we will not forget that conversion is only the beginning of the Christian life.

1. *New Christians Need Guidance*

New Christians—new young Christians especially—need a great deal of help in knowing what it means to live as Christians, to think as Christians. We so frequently see Juniors whose understanding is as limited as that of James and John when they asked the Master to destroy the Samaritan village. Like the sons of Zebedee they "know not what . . . spirit" they are of (Luke 9:55). A teacher's responsibility is never finished when he has led a pupil to trust Jesus as Saviour. One great, important phase of that responsibility is just beginning.

2. *Jesus Commanded the Teaching of New Converts*

We have the authority of Jesus for that. In the Great Commission Jesus charged his followers that they were to "teach all nations, *baptizing* them—" and that after their converts were baptized, they were to go on teaching them. Teaching them what? "All things whatsoever I have commanded you." Every lesson we teach should help the Christians in our classes get a deeper understanding of what it means to live every day as Christians.

3. *Christian Living the Best Witness*

I heard of a minister who closed his sermon with a sincere and moving appeal. All week he had hoped and prayed that this might be the day when some heart would be stirred to make a profession of faith. To his great joy someone *did* respond, a man who had been on the hearts and in the prayers of minister and members for a long time.

Sometime later, when the minister came to know that new member better, he had an opportunity to ask a question—one that had puzzled him for some time. "Tell me," he said; "you had heard me preach so often before that morning. What was it I said in that particular sermon that helped open your heart to the call of the Lord Jesus when none of my other pleas had succeeded?"

Quietly the man replied, "It was nothing you said in that particular sermon. The thing that led me to want to know Jesus better was the life of a Christian I know. I saw what faith in Christ did for his life, and I wanted for myself the thing that blessed his life. Your words showed me the way; his life led me to seek the way."

It is a teacher's great opportunity to help his Christian Juniors understand that the way a Christian acts is one of the ways he has of witnessing, of helping others to want to know more about Jesus. That is surely what Jesus had in mind when he said, "By their fruits ye shall know them."

LET'S THINK

1. Just as Jesus said that all the commandments could be summed up in two great ones, so all the purposes of Junior Sunday school work can be summed in two great statements. What are they?

2. When a Junior teacher goes into his classroom on Sunday morning, he may say, "I have an opportunity greater than anyone else in the Sunday school this morning to win to Christ." Why does a Junior teacher almost without exception have an opportunity to win more pupils to Christ than teachers of older age groups? Younger age groups? Why is his opportunity greater than that of the pastor? The department superintendent? Many parents?

3. Give three reasons why it is so important to win Juniors to Christ *while they are Juniors*.

4. Study the action words in the Great Commission (Matt. 28:19-20): "Go . . . teach . . . baptizing . . . teaching." What do these words suggest that Jesus thought necessary before and after winning converts?

WHO SHOULD TEACH JUNIORS?

The teacher teaches what he is; that is why it is so important that he be what he teaches.

Outline

I. A TEACHER MUST BELIEVE IN CERTAIN FUNDAMENTALS

  1. A Teacher Must Believe in Sunday School Teaching
  2. A Teacher Must Believe in Boys and Girls
  3. A Teacher Must Believe in the Book He Teaches
  4. A Teacher Must Believe in Prayer
  5. A Teacher Must Believe in Jesus.

II. A TEACHER SHOULD BE WILLING TO WORK

III. A TEACHER SHOULD BE WILLING TO LEARN

IV. A TEACHER SHOULD BE DEPENDABLE

V. A TEACHER SHOULD BE CO-OPERATIVE

VI. A TEACHER SHOULD BE YOUNG IN HEART

VII. OTHER QUALIFICATIONS

CHAPTER II

WHO SHOULD TEACH JUNIORS?

How many of the Sunday school teachers you had as a child can you remember? One or two or three? What makes you remember those certain ones? Is it the lessons they taught? The experiences they shared with you? Or is it just something about the teachers themselves?

If you are like most adults, you cannot recall specific lessons taught by those long-ago teachers. What you remember is the teacher, the quality of his personality, the kind of human being he was. You are like the man who said, "Mr. Farmer was the greatest teacher I ever had. I don't remember much that Mr. Farmer taught; I just remember—Mr. Farmer."

In Sunday school teaching, nothing counts so much as what the teacher *is,* the things he believes, the aims that motivate his teaching. One reason is that the teacher never entirely separates himself from the lesson he teaches. Whether he wills it or not, the lesson will come to the pupil bearing something of the teacher himself, the marks of his outlook, his convictions, his sincerity. The teacher teaches what he *is;* that is why it is so important that he *be* what he teaches.

WHAT ARE THE REQUIREMENTS FOR
A TEACHER OF JUNIORS?

What are the qualities that a good teacher of Juniors should have—or cultivate? We will not be concerned in this chapter with skills and techniques of teaching; those matters will come later. Right now we are thinking of the basic qualities, the essentials that determine a man or woman's eligibility to teach.

I. A Teacher Must Believe in Certain Fundamentals

1. *A Teacher Must Believe in Sunday School Teaching*

When I say "believe in Sunday school teaching," I do not mean "acknowledge verbally that Sunday school teaching is important." I mean have a deep underlying conviction that helping boys and girls become followers of Jesus and grow in Christian living is the most important task in which any adult can invest his time. I mean a feeling that Sunday school teaching has consequences in Juniors' lives for right now, for the future, and for eternity. "With the help of Jesus, my teaching can change Juniors—and changed boys and girls are what it takes to make a changed tomorrow."

That is the sort of believing it takes—an active, dynamic conviction that gives drive and direction to study; that charges teaching with purpose and power; that lights up the little routine tasks—the letter-writing, the visiting, the telephoning, the record-studying—with the glow of a high motive, a sure goal.

(1) *Weekdays are opportunities, too.*—A teacher's belief in Sunday school teaching must be so secure that it will not be shaken by the criticism sometimes voiced: "But what can you do in one hour a week?"

In the first place, a dedicated teacher does not confine his teaching to "one hour a week." Good teachers find ways to extend their teaching through every day of the week. They give their pupils weekday activities related to the Sunday school lessons. They check up on the outcome of these activities. Class meetings, visits, letters, outdoor get-togethers—all these opportunities for through-the-week contacts strengthen Sunday morning teaching.

The Sunday morning hour can be extended by enlisting parents as weekday assistants to the teacher. A

Sunday school teacher cannot be on hand to see how the things he taught on Sunday meet the test of living on Monday—but the parents can. Through parent meetings, visits, letters, the use of class mothers, personal counseling, and parent sponsors, teachers can line them up as teammates.

What can you do in seventy-five minutes on Sunday? A believing teacher will respond:

"I can do a great deal. While trying in every way possible to lengthen my Sunday morning time, I will let no man despise my Sunday morning minutes. Lives have been changed in five minutes of time and two words were all that were required to start James and John, Peter and Andrew down a new road of life dedication for the rest of their lives. I will use my teaching time to help my Juniors know that Jesus still says to boys and girls, men and women, 'Follow me,' and to help them hear and accept that invitation, and then be followers in the way they live and act."

(2) *A teacher follows the example of Jesus.*—When Jesus faced his lifework, he chose to give teaching a major emphasis in his plan. "You call me Teacher and Lord; and you are right, for so I am" (John 13:13 RSV). Jesus selected a little group of pupils. He held school in the literal meaning of that term. He taught lessons. Those lessons he enriched and invigorated through the use of the attractive and compelling methods that we today term "modern" teaching techniques. He taught visually and dramatically. He taught through discussion and questions and answers. He told stories. He used pupil activity; his pupils learned to do by doing.

And when, in the end, he turned his work over to those he had trained, he left them in no doubt as to how they were to carry it on by helping people become Christians—by *teaching* these new Christians to observe all things whatsoever their Teacher had commanded.

2. A Teacher Must Believe in Boys and Girls

(1) *All children are important.*—No one should dare to teach who does not respect the worth and dignity of boys and girls. This means all boys and girls, not just the bright and satisfactory ones who reward our efforts here and now, but those other children, the unresponsive, the uninterested, the slow to understand—those whom we call "problem Juniors." For the Christian teacher these boys and girls should present the strongest appeal, the highest challenge, for when children are most unlovable they need love the most; when they are most un-understandable, they need understanding the most. A Christian teacher should remember always that there are no problem Juniors; there are only Juniors with problems.

(2) *Children have a right to be children.*—Respect for boys and girls means respecting their right to *be* boys and girls. There are adults who look on childhood as a stretch of life to be lived through, tolerated, until adulthood, when life really begins. We know now that the experiences a child undergoes at five or at ten are as important to him at five or at ten as are the experiences he will undergo at thirty or forty or fifty.

(3) *The possibility of change is greatest in childhood.*—If a teacher's attitude toward his pupils is patterned on Jesus', he will believe in his pupils for what they may become. He will look at pupils-as-they-are—the Junior Peters and Zacchaeuses and Matthews—and see in them the people they may become.

For teachers of boys and girls the vision is always a hopeful one, for they work with life at that stage when the possibility of change is so great. A Junior's habits have not yet hardened into a way of life. His choices can still be guided, his ideals influenced. "Just as the *twig* is bent, the tree's inclined."

It is told of the old teacher of Martin Luther that he always bowed low whenever he came into the presence of a new class of boys. "I never forget," he explained, "that I might be in the presence of one who is greater than my emperor." There is always that might-be when we work with boys and girls.

> The hand that is busy with playthings now
> The reins of power will hold.
> And it matters so much how we guide him today,
> The boy who is twelve years old.

3. *A Teacher Must Believe in the Book He Teaches*

A teacher of Juniors must be one who believes that the Bible is God's Book, given to men that they might know him better, that they might believe on his Son, that they might have a guide for living in this world.

A little native boy in a central Congo village sat listening with fixed gaze as the missionary read from the Scriptures. As soon as the service was finished, he hastened to the missionary and asked "Oh, sir, may I have that book, so that I may read it to the people of my village off in the forest? Those words made holes in my heart."

(1) *A teacher needs experiences with the Bible.*— Something of that kind of sincerity must stir the teacher who shares the Bible with boys and girls. "I believe this is God's Book because I have found God here on its pages. I believe its principles work out in life because they have worked in my life; I know its promises are true because they have never failed me in my need."

Nothing can shake a Bible-faith arrived at by such a route.

(2) *A teacher needs to grow in Bible knowledge.*—A teacher's belief in the Bible is strengthened by familiarity with its contents. It is not enough for a teacher to read

the Bible to get his Sunday school lesson from it, to study only enough to pass on to his pupils. He must read it regularly, devotionally for his own spiritual nourishment. And the teacher who does that discovers a surprising truth: The Bible passages that he studies, meditates on through the week will somehow show through in next Sunday's lesson, even though he never mentions those passages in that lesson.

Some Junior teachers find that using for their daily Bible readings the lesson passages they are to teach not only gives daily devotional help, but enriches the passages for their teaching. Some have found that the memory passages offer a fine source of devotional readings. Such a practice lifts "memory work" from word-teaching to experience-sharing. (For a further discussion of the teacher and his Bible, see chapter 7.)

4. *A Teacher Must Believe in Prayer*

We cannot help our Juniors build a lifelong friendship with God if we ourselves have not cultivated him as Friend. We cannot enrich any other person's conception of God beyond our own.

A teacher must pray because he needs strength beyond his own in his problems as a teacher. It is not enough for a teacher to pray, "God help my class." None of us teaches a class. We teach Jerry and Sally and Ronnie and Hugh. And we must pray for Jerry and Sally and the others as people, with full awareness of their individual problems and needs.

And here is a miracle that every teacher who "prays believing" has experienced: When we pray for Jerry, we ourselves discover a fresh insight into Jerry's problems. Because of our praying, God will help Jerry directly—we have his promise for that—but he also helps *us*, the human agent through whom he works, to understand better how to help Jerry.

5. *A Teacher Must Believe in Jesus*

We have already pointed out the indispensability of this requirement for one who seeks to win Juniors to Christ. (See page 11.) But what do we mean when we say a Sunday school teacher must "believe in" Jesus?

Believing in Jesus means believing that he is God's Son, with power to save from sin. It means trusting him as personal Saviour.

Believing in Jesus means believing that he is actively at work in the world today—at work through the Holy Spirit, at work strengthening and comforting those who follow him, at work opening hearts to hear and heed his call, at work helping followers make the right choices and stand bravely in times of temptation.

Believing in Jesus means believing in the principles that he taught, even those principles that might conflict with our cherished prejudices and deep-rooted biases. "Why call ye me, Lord, Lord," Jesus asked one time, "and do not the things which I say?" (Luke 6:46). Believing in Jesus means daring to submit every attitude, every line of conduct to the inflexible test: What did Jesus teach about this? How did Jesus feel? What would he do?

So far we have considered the factors that make a man or woman eligible to teach—the prospective teacher's "entrance requirements." There are other necessary qualities he should have—or seek to have.

II. A TEACHER SHOULD BE WILLING TO WORK

Anyone enlisting a Junior teacher should be honest enough to warn: This is going to take work. To prepare and teach a good lesson takes work. To visit, hold class meetings, support the weekly meetings takes work. Prospective teachers need to be warned as solemnly as young couples embarking on married life are warned by their minister that the task they face is a serious one, and not to be "entered into unadvisedly or lightly, but reverently, discreetly, advisedly, soberly, and in the fear of God."

Nor is a teacher of Graded Lessons, one who teaches the same lessons over and over, to think that increasing experience and familiarity with the lessons releases him from the necessity of hard work. *The lessons are old, but the Juniors are new,* and each new class of Juniors demands that the teacher restudy the Bible passages in the light of their special needs and capacities.

To the teacher who invests heavily of time and thought in his work comes a happy discovery: The harder he works, the easier is his work! Lack of response on the part of pupils, irregular attendance, discipline problems —all these obstacles to effective teaching can so often be traced to insufficient preparation, lack of Bible background, inadequate pupil-knowledge. The teacher who gives himself without stint to being a teacher discovers anew the old, old law of the harvest: A bountiful reaping is possible only when there has been a bountiful sowing.

III. A Teacher Should Be Willing to Learn

"Who dares to be a teacher must never cease to be a pupil." For a Sunday school teacher there can never be a graduation day, a day when he can say: "My study time is over. I know enough." A teacher of Juniors must constantly seek to extend his Bible knowledge, his understanding of boys and girls, his awareness of what is going on in the world. It helps if he has some understanding, too, of what is going on in the world of public-school education.

The books prepared for workers in the Sunday school and Training Union offer teachers a balanced plan of study. A church fortunate enough to have a library can offer its teachers resources for improving their minds.

IV. A Teacher Should Be Dependable

"She has some fine traits—but I never could depend on her." Many of us have heard a superintendent say that about some teacher—and with those words write the epitaph to that teacher's usefulness.

Dependability is a quality of simple integrity. A dependable teacher has an old-fashioned respect for duty and a wholesome respect for himself—too much respect to do a shoddy job. A dependable teacher respects the contract that he has made with his church, with himself, with his Lord—a contract entered into when he promised to be a teacher of boys or girls.

It is not going too far to say that a teacher who is not dependable is a not-quite-honest person.

A dependable teacher will certainly be as conscientious about his Sunday morning job as he is about his weekday job. He will not let some trivial circumstance interfere with meeting his class on Sunday. He will notify his superintendent as soon as possible when he finds that he cannot be present. He will do the necessary visiting and attend the meetings of the Junior workers. He will give enough time to his study to be able to guide a good lesson. "O Timothy, keep that which is committed to thy trust," a veteran teacher wrote a young one long ago (1 Tim. 6:20). A Sunday school teacher has a trust, and he should be strong enough to keep that trust which has been committed to him by God.

V. A Teacher Should Be Co-operative

A teacher should recognize that he and his pupils are more than a class; they are part of the whole school—

of the church itself. So often the best interests of the whole group demand that a teacher or class put other interests above their own as, for example, when a small class is asked to surrender its room to a larger class, or a large class is requested to release some of its good members to start another class.

A co-operating teacher will respect the Sunday school's ruling about grading, about the hour for teachers to arrive. He will be in the assembly periods, but he will do more; he will participate in those services. He will worship.

When a teacher co-operates with his Sunday school—when he supports the officers and teachers' meetings, attends the preaching services without fail; when he shows enthusiasm for the total program of his church—he is teaching a far more vivid lesson than he will ever teach in words. He is *being* a doer of the Word!

VI. A TEACHER SHOULD BE YOUNG IN HEART

A Junior teacher should be young—but not necessarily young in years. Youthfulness is a matter of spirit, of outlook—not of calendar years. There are old people of twenty-five and delightfully young people of sixty-five.

How old are you? The more of the following questions to which you can answer yes, the more likely you are to have the youthfulness that a good Junior teacher needs.

Do I refuse to let Juniors' high spirits irritate me?
Do I *laugh with* my Juniors (never at them)?
Am I willing to change my plans on short notice?
Do boys and girls seek my company?
Do I enjoy sharing my Juniors' social life?
Do I speak to a Junior in his own language?
Am I adaptable?
Do I go on learning, growing, stretching my mind?

VII. OTHER QUALIFICATIONS

Of course there are many, many other fine qualities that Junior teachers should have, or seek to have. Cheerfulness, patience, humility—these are so important, and so are loyalty and emotional balance and a sense of humor. It would be impossible to name all the desirable qualities.

Fortunately, a teacher who nourishes his spiritual life through Bible study and prayer and worship in church, a teacher who practices his Christianity can grow in those fine traits that increase his effectiveness. There are no "born teachers." Teachers are born, someone has said, but they are not "born made." They make themselves.

This chapter is called "Who Should Teach Juniors?" In raising that question at the very beginning of this book, I have tried to underscore the fact that the teacher himself is the most important factor in teaching, and that what he himself is—the way he feels and thinks and acts —speaks more loudly than anything he ever says.

Some Sunday school lessons are *spoken*. Some Sunday school lessons are *lived*. But a Sunday school lesson *spoken* and then backed up by a Sunday school lesson *lived* is irresistible. Only out of such a combination will great Sunday school teaching grow.

LET'S THINK

1. Which do you think teaches more vividly, what a teacher says or what he lives? What responsibility does that put on Sunday school teachers?

2. Think of one teacher of your acquaintance (or one who has taught you), a teacher whom you believe to be successful. Measure him (or her) by the qualifications listed in this chapter. Now measure yourself as a teacher by those qualifications.

3. Why should a teacher of Juniors be one who has actually had an experience of conversion?

4. What significance does this saying have for teachers of boys and girls: "As the twig is bent, so the tree's inclined"?

THESE ARE YOUR JUNIORS

We realize that just knowing *what* he teaches is not enough; the teacher must know equally as well *those* he teaches. The human material with which he works is as much the teacher's sphere of study as the printed material.

Outline

I. The Growing Emphasis on the Pupil

II. Who Are People Called Juniors?

1. Juniors Are Doers
2. Juniors Are Discovering the World
3. Juniors Are Emerging from Childhood
4. Some of the Interests of Boys and Girls Are Diverging
5. Juniors Are Old Enough to Choose Between Right and Wrong

III. These Are Junior Purposes

1. In Relation to the Bible
2. In Relation to the Church
3. In Relation to Jesus
4. In Relation to the Home
5. In Relation to Others

Chapter III

THESE ARE YOUR JUNIORS

I. The Growing Emphasis on the Pupil

An old-time rule for teachers was in the form of a little rhyme:

> You cannot lead where you do not go.
> You cannot teach what you do not know.

That was—and still is—a good rule. Teachers must know the "what" of teaching—their subject matter—before they can lead others to know it.

The trouble was, in those earlier days, the subject matter was the *only* thing that counted. Let a teacher master his book, people seemed to think, and he had mastered the art of teaching.

As we have grown in our understanding of how people learn, we have broadened our thinking about what teaching involves. We realize now that just knowing *what* he teaches is not enough; the teacher must know equally as well *those he teaches.* The human material with which he works is as much the teacher's sphere of study as the printed material. Many good Bible students have failed in helping Juniors to understand and appreciate the Bible because they knew the Bible only; they didn't know Juniors.

Our growing realization of the importance of the pupil has grown out of a better understanding of what teaching is. Teaching is not just transmitting facts. Teaching is guiding changes in boys and girls (see chapter 4). We might borrow Paul's phraseology and say, "And how then can we change boys and girls except we know boys and girls? And how can we know boys and girls except we study them?"

II. WHO ARE PEOPLE CALLED JUNIORS?

In this study of how to teach, we will do the very thing we urge teachers to begin the study of a lesson by doing. We will spend some time in thoughtful, searching study of people called Juniors. We will not forget, as we study children in general, that there are no "general" children. Jerry Jones is like nobody else in the world, and the only way to know Jerry is to study Jerry—his home, his play life, his hobbies and interests, his Sunday school records.

However, understanding that certain characteristics are common to normal children of the same age helps teachers know what to expect of children, to anticipate problems, interpret the behavior they observe. It reminds them that there aren't any new problems; there are just old problems happening to new teachers.

The teacher who understands that certain behavior is normal for a certain age is more apt to take a sane, constructive view of that behavior.

1. *Juniors Are Doers*

(1) *Juniors are doers in their physical lives.*—A superintendent faced her Junior group. "How many of you would like to——"

At that point—before she finished her sentence—every hand in the room was frantically waving. "I would, let me, let me," the hands were saying.

The Juniors did not know what the superintendent was going to suggest that they do—but that did not matter. They just wanted to *do!*

If we had to mention the trait most characteristic of Juniors, it would perhaps be this: Juniors are *doers*. Not sitters, not hearers only, but *doers*.

A healthy child of any age is active, but it does seem that during Junior years the hunger to *do*—to busy the whole of self, hands and feet and legs and mind, every waking moment—possesses the child completely. "He never walks when he can run, nor runs when he can dash or leap," a mother said of her nine-year-old. This is a time when pent-up nervous energy demands almost constant expression in activities.

Physical factors are largely responsible. A normal Junior enjoys good health. During early Junior years, growth levels off and continues slow and steady until along in the twelfth year, when the preadolescent growth-spurt sets in. Resistance to disease is higher in Junior years than in any other period of childhood. The Metropolitan Life Insurance Company tells us that the eleventh year is the safest year of life—the year when fewer deaths occur than in any other.

Sound nerves, good appetites, disease-free bodies add up to a sense of well-being that is certain to boil over into an excess of energy.

(2) *Juniors are doers in their mental lives.*—Nor is the Junior's energy confined to physical life. His mind too "wants to go." Puzzles, riddles, conundrums, quizzes, and contests delight him; they give his eager mind a workout. Juniors are soaking up impressions and information from every source their environment offers—from advertisements, the radio, comic books, television, newspapers, the conversation of adults, the sermons they hear, the teaching of the Sunday school.

Impressive statistics and facts of interest gleaned from all these sources are stored in memory to be sprung on the first audience willing to listen. "Bet you don't know how many tons of water a tree draws up through its leaves every day." "Do you know how long it would take a jet plane to get to the moon?" "Guess how long it took the Bible to get written."

Rhymes and jingles also have charm, and are memorized eagerly, then recited without urging.

(3) *We must meet the Junior's need to do.*—What does all this mean to Sunday school teachers? That they must plan lessons that allow their Juniors to be doers. The great failure of most lessons worked out by Junior teachers is that they provide more opportunity for teachers to do than for pupils to do. A good Junior lesson crackles with activities—with problems to think through, discussions, quizzes, picture games, and brain-challenging ways to get the Bible studied.

A word of warning: These activities should be on the Junior's interest-level. To propose activities that are more suitable for younger children is to forfeit the Junior's respect and alienate his interest.

"I must do things; I am made that way. If you don't plan things for me to do, I will plan them." No, your Junior won't tell you that in words; he will tell you in a more vivid way: by his behavior. Problem behavior is just pupil activity that teachers have not directed to purposeful ends. The cure for it? *Give the Juniors something better to do:*

"Paste one of these flags on the map in each place you find Paul visiting in today's lesson."

"This picture shows three things mentioned in today's lesson. Watch for them as you read the Bible."

"Here are pencils and paper. Write the name of a blessing God has given you today."

If the teacher works at it, he can provide activities attractive enough to compete with the undesirable ones that the Juniors usually plan when left to themselves.

2. *Juniors Are Discovering the World*

(1) *The world of space.*—Draw a map of the little child's world, and it is no bigger than the four walls of home. With every year of growing, the child's world grows a little too. By the time he reaches Junior years—in some cases, mid-Junior years, his world takes in the

universe. He has discovered oceans and continents; can point to North, South, East and West; can read a map and has a good idea of where he is in the world of space.

Proud of his newly acquired map skills, the Junior will eagerly whirl a globe to find the spot where some relative has visited, or perhaps the place discussed in last Sunday's Sunday school lesson.

The people of the world are even more fascinating. Juniors are interested in details of the everyday life of people of other times, other lands—their dress, habits, customs as well as their ideas and attitudes.

This growing world-awareness makes the Junior years a peculiarly appropriate time to teach missions, to help Juniors acquire a sense of Christian stewardship. It is a time to teach Christlike attitudes of brotherly love and understanding toward all people of all races and nations. "If Christ died for all men, then I can consider no man of less worth or importance than I"—that is something Juniors need to believe.

(2) *The world of time.*—A child of five lives in the here and now. He cannot comprehend not being alive or of anyone having lived before him. By the time he is nine or ten, he has acquired some time sense. Not only can he tell time by the clock and calendar, but he can comprehend the idea of a past and present; he has some grasp of historic time.

Do you see what this means to teachers? The Junior now has a background for comprehending the unfolding story of the Bible. He is ready to understand the significance of its Testaments, the before-Jesus part and the after-Jesus part. He can begin to place Bible events and characters in their proper place in Bible history. He can understand something of God's large plan to send Jesus— a plan beginning in the dawn of time.

(3) *The world of ideas.*—Of all the new worlds opening up to Juniors, the most exciting—and the most dis-

turbing—is the world of ideas. Through radio, news-papers, adult conversations, discussions in school, Juniors are learning that the way people think—the convictions they hold—constitutes a force of vast importance in the world. Wars are fought and governments are formed and laws are made—because ideas get hold of people.

Increasingly aware of the conflict of opinions, of an-tagonisms between class and class, nation and nation, Juniors are asking, "What makes one group think one thing and another group think another thing? Which is the right way to think? Which way should I think?"

This new sensitiveness to ideas makes these Junior years a time when attitudes toward people and things are easily caught. Teachers should examine their own to see if they square with "Love thy neighbour as thy self," "Judge not, that ye be not judged." "Do good to them that hate you," and all the other high principles that Jesus taught governing human relationships.

And when discussions arise in class, the teacher must realize that the only infallible authority is God's own Word. Wise is the teacher who knows his Bible so well that he can suggest in the course of any discussion, "Let's see what God's Word says about that."

3. *Juniors Are Emerging from Childhood*

When does childhood end? The Junior years mark the last frontier of childhood. It is during these four Junior years that boys and girls are literally "putting away childish things" that is, the symbols and the play interests of childhood—dolls, games like "cops and robbers and G-men." Most children have "put away" belief in Santa Claus by the time they are nine.

Juniors are loosening the apron strings. A younger child will ask, "Mother, may I go over and play with Charles?" But a Junior will announce: "Mother, I'm going over and play with Charles. It's O.K., isn't it?"

In Sunday school we must recognize that. We never address Juniors as "little folks" or "children." Juniors are capable of assuming responsibilities beyond the ability of Primary children. They can function as class officers. They can plan their own parties. They can enlist other Juniors in Sunday school. They can beautify their classrooms. They can help plan programs.

Juniors are growing up in every area. They are mature enough so that they can set themselves to a task and see it through to completion. They no longer have to wait for an adult to take the initiative in starting them on lessons or assigned activities. Juniors are "self-starters." It is in the fourth grade that homework begins to be effective and meaningful.

Juniors have gained sufficient skills in reading so that words are now a means to an end; they are tools which a child can use to get the sense behind the words on a page. By the time he is ten a child can skim a written page for thought and search for the main idea of a story.

Up until the Junior years, the Sunday school lesson material is cast in the form of a Bible story, which the teacher tells and to which the child listens. But in a Junior class, the boys and girls read the lesson passage directly from the Bible. This ability to use their Bibles in class and assembly is, for Sunday school workers, one of the most important differences between Juniors and younger children.

4. Some of the Interests of Boys and Girls Are Diverging

As boys and girls enter the mid-Junior years, their interests show increasing divergence. Dr. Arnold Gesell tells us: "At ten years, sex differences are pronounced. The psychology of a 10-year-old girl is significantly distinguishable from that of a 10-year-old boy of equivalent breeding and experience. This difference appears to be fundamental."[1]

(1) *Juniors prefer their own sex.*—This growing difference results in a drawing apart of the sexes, each sex preferring its own company, especially in games and other activities. Watch a group of Juniors at a Junior social and notice how they group for play. It is almost always on the basis of boys with boys and girls with girls. Commenting on this characteristic Dr. Gesell says: "At seven years a boy and girl may pair off as playmates for a period of weeks or months, but the larger play groupings generally ignore sex lines. In another year boys and girls begin to separate in their play; and from nine years to the teens there is a definite period of segregation."[2]

That is not to say, however, that boys do not have "girl friends" and vice versa. Especially is this true in the eleventh and twelfth years. Boys are a major topic of interest in *groups* of girls in those years. But the interest is superficial rather than real, and usually is for the purpose of making the girl herself look important in the eyes of her friends.

(2) *Separate classes for boys and girls.*—These things being true, it is much better to separate boys and girls for Bible teaching in the Sunday school. There are fewer discipline problems in an all-girl or an all-boy class than in a mixed class, and better attention in class.

But the basic reason for separating boys and girls for Bible teaching in Junior classes is that we teach Sunday school lessons for living, and already life is beginning to be different for boys and girls. A teacher planning a lesson for boys will use a different "interest-getter" for his opening from that used by a teacher planning that same

[1] Arnold Gesell and Frances, L. Ilg, *The Child from Five to Ten*, (New York: Harper and Brothers, 1946), pp. 213, 337. Used by permission.
[2] Ibid., p. 237. Used by permission.

lesson for girls. A teacher of boys will draw his illustrations from different areas of life; he might apply his lessons in a different way to everyday living.

(3) *Men teachers for boys, women for girls.*—Another major point in our Junior program grows out of the basic differences between boys and girls: It is better for men to teach boys and women to teach girls. "But men do not keep up with modern educational methods as well as women do," some workers object. "And they do not go in for creative activities as women do."

Even if that claim were true, it is better for a class of boys to have a man as a teacher. A man is teaching a boy—silently but vividly—a lesson that no woman living could teach: Sunday school is important for men as well as for women. "One example is worth a hundred exhortations."

The widowed mother of a nine-year-old said to his Junior superintendent, "I cannot tell you what it means to my boy to have a man for a teacher. His Sunday school teacher is the only man he has any real contact with." The influence of a Christian man is a need in the life of every boy.

We might sum all this up: The reason boys need men as teachers is—boys grow up to *be* men!

5. *Juniors Are Old Enough to Choose Between Right and Wrong*

Most boys and girls by the time they are nine are old enough to choose between right and wrong, old enough to know what sin is and to realize that "all have sinned and come short of the glory of God." We believe that when that is true, boys and girls are ready to make the greatest choice: to choose Jesus as Saviour.

We are not saying that evangelistic teaching begins in the Junior years. Every lesson the child has learned about Jesus from earliest years has, in a sense, been evangelistic—if it has contributed to his love and appreciation of Jesus. But in these earlier years the teachers were seeking to lead the child *toward* Jesus. In Junior years teachers should seek to lead them *to* Jesus.

III. THESE ARE JUNIOR PURPOSES

We are ready now to think about the purposes toward which we will work, the objectives our Juniors are ready for. Having set a Junior in the midst and studied him carefully, we are ready to think in specific terms, to answer the question: What can we reasonably expect to accomplish with boys and girls in Sunday school when they are nine, ten, eleven, and twelve?

For studying these purposes, we have organized them around some key words.

1. *In Relation to the Bible.*—During Junior years we want our boys and girls to have *experiences* with the Bible. We want them to read it to find the help it has for them, to read it to enjoy its interesting stories. In order to handle the Bible with ease and pleasure, Juniors must learn the names of the books of the Bible, the names of the groupings, and the order in which these come. That is one of the purposes on which we focus.

We want our Juniors to grow in the belief that the Bible is God's inspired Word, given to men that they might first believe that Jesus is the Christ, the Son of God, and that believing they might have life through his name. We want them to know that God gave his Book to help people understand how to live with others wisely and well, that it is a guidebook, a lamp to their feet and a light to their path. We want our Juniors to form the habit of daily Bible reading. We want them to memorize portions of the Bible—and to understand what they memorize.

2. *In Relation to the Church.*—During Junior years we want Juniors to become members of the church after an experience of conversion; we want them to form the habit of regular church attendance and to grow in the ability to concentrate on the sermon and to take part in each part of the service. Our goal now is not just *attendance,* but better attention. We want Juniors to grow in the feeling that the church is *their* church and that they have a responsibility for supporting its services and its program for spreading the gospel.

3. *In Relation to Jesus.*—During Junior years we want our Juniors to commit their lives to Jesus as their Saviour and Lord. We want them to know that "there is none other name under heaven given among men, whereby we must be saved" (Acts 4:12). Relying on the Bible and working with the Holy Spirit, we will seek to help them to trust him as Saviour and look to him as their Guide and Example in everyday living, and to have a growing feeling of responsibility for sharing their knowledge of Jesus with all people.

4. *In Relation to the Home.*—During Junior years we want our Juniors to follow the example of Jesus in being obedient in their homes. We want them to grow in the ability to do their part in making their homes happy and harmonious and to accept cheerfully their share of responsibility.

5. *In Relation to Others.*—In Junior years we should help our boys and girls to grow in the ability to be Christian in their attitude toward others, to depend on Jesus to help them be more and more unselfish and considerate. We should help them know that it is Christian to respect the rights of *all* people, even those who differ from us in race and class; to remember that Jesus died to save all people, not just a favored few. During Junior years we want our boys and girls to feel a sense of re-

sponsibility for helping others know about Jesus—those in their families, their neighborhoods, their towns, and those in the uttermost part of the earth.

LET'S THINK

1. Select one Junior and study him for five minutes when he does not know that he is being observed. It may be on a bus, at an entertainment, or in the home. Notice the number and variety of movements he makes. Count them. What one word do you think describes the Junior better than any other?

2. The following facts are true of Juniors. Name one thing a Sunday school teacher does for his Juniors because each of these facts is true.

Juniors are active in their bodies.

Juniors are active in their minds.

Interests of Junior boys and girls are different.

Juniors are old enough to choose between right and wrong.

3. Tell at least one purpose you think a Junior teacher should work toward in each of these areas: The Bible, the church, Jesus, the home, other people.

HOW JUNIORS LEARN

People who build houses must learn something of the nature of wood and brick and stone and mortar. People who grow vegetables must find out how peas and carrots and radishes grow. And men and women who teach boys and girls—really teach them—must have some insight into the way their minds work—the way they learn.

Outline

CHAPTER IV

HOW JUNIORS LEARN

The man was young, very troubled, and very much in earnest. He had waited until the last worker had left the conference room to talk to me. "Do you think a teacher ought to resign if he isn't getting anywhere with his class?" he asked. I asked him why he thought he was not getting anywhere.

The young teacher started talking then, telling me what went on in his classroom each Sunday morning. The picture *was* discouraging. But it was not as black— or as unusual—as he thought.

"The boys don't listen to me more than three or four minutes," he declared; "then they start doing something else. I have been teaching two months last Sunday, and do you know how many times I have been able to reach the climax in my lesson? Not one time. I usually don't get beyond my second point."

"What do the Juniors do?" I asked.

He shook his head. "Everything but listen. Sometimes they get up and go over to the window, or start picking on one another. Sometimes they interrupt me to ask a question that hasn't got anything to do with what I'm saying. That really throws me off the track! Sometimes one will tell a story on some other subject entirely."

I asked him to tell me something about how he taught, how he guided his lesson discussion. "I get up a pretty good lesson," he answered, "or it would be good if I ever had a chance to teach it. I spend hours studying. I read reference books. I do research at the library. What is wrong?"

What *was* wrong? Can you guess? I think the teacher himself has told us unconsciously.

In the first place, his idea of teaching was talking—
a teacher talking. Notice, "They don't *listen* more than
three minutes," and "They do everything but *listen*." The
teacher was proceeding on the old theory of "You sit
still while I instill."

The teacher was teaching in a stiff, formal way—
preaching a sermon, probably, more than teaching a
lesson. He allowed for no give-and-take between pupils
and teacher, no adjustment to the interests and needs of
the pupils as they were revealed through discussion:
"I never reach my climax." "I do not get beyond my
second point." "They throw me off the track."

The teacher was giving his pupils no chance to *do*
things: "They walk around." "They interrupt to ask a
question." "They start telling a story." How much those
boys wanted to *do!* How vividly they were begging to
be *used!*

The teacher was preparing lessons, not with the interests and needs of Juniors in mind—but with those of
adults! "They ask questions not related to the lessons."
"They will start telling a story on some other subject."
The lesson was not touching Junior life at any point.

Perhaps we could sum up the teacher's whole trouble
by saying that he was teaching *lessons*, not pupils. He
had never taken the trouble to find out how peoples'
minds work, how they learn.

Teachers do not drive automobiles without finding out
how automobiles run. They do not build houses without
learning something about the nature of wood and
brick and stone and mortar. They do not plant gardens
without finding out how peas and carrots and radishes
grow. Yet they will undertake to teach Juniors without
finding out about the laws by which they learn.

For there are laws governing the way people learn
just as there are laws governing the way plants grow—
and machines run.

Before we examine these laws, let me say that there are many fine and effective teachers who have never heard of the laws of learning. But these teachers are working in harmony with them, even though they are doing so unconsciously. They are men and women who have such a keen understanding of human nature that they instinctively do the right thing, the effective thing, the thing that gets results in their teaching.

Perhaps we should not even call these great human principles "laws," for that term suggests something dry and bookish, something far removed from the everyday world in which we live. Actually the laws of learning are just statements of certain universal truths regarding the way people act and react. Down through the ages people have observed that certain ways of teaching work and that others do not. When a certain thing is true about most people most of the time, we may call that truth a law.

I. THE LAW OF READINESS

The first law of learning is the law of readiness. The textbooks state it like this: When one is ready to act in a certain way, to act is pleasant and not to act is annoying.

1. *How the Law Works*

We have all observed the working of that law in our own experience, whether we have recognized or labeled it as a "law" or not. Here is an example, one you could match with others out of your own experience almost daily.

At this moment I am deeply interested in writing this chapter. If someone should ask me to leave it and commence at once an article on home-church co-operation (to name one subject), the suggestion would be anything but welcome. My interests are so wrapped around this topic, my faculties so concentrated upon it, that it would take me at least a day to "warm up" to any other subject—even one I consider just as important.

I am ready for this task—and not for any other.

This does not mean that with ourselves or with our pupils we will pamper selfish preferences. It does not mean that people should do exactly what they want to do. Circumstances often demand that we leave something in which we are extremely interested and concentrate on something entirely different.

What I am saying here is that people, old and young, learn more quickly, perform more efficiently when the thing they are learning or creating is something for which they feel a need, mental, spiritual, or emotional, something for which they are *ready*.

Examples of this principle are all around you. The teacher cannot get a boy to take any interest at all in geography—until his father goes overseas. Then suddenly faraway countries take on a new fascination, and he explores maps and books to find out all he can about Korea or Japan or Alaska. I heard of a second-grade boy just recently who took no interest at all in reading the words in his reader; his teacher labeled him a nonreader. Then he got interested in making model airplanes—and learned very quickly how to read the directions he needed to pursue his hobby. He was *ready* for reading then.

2. *The Law at Work in Sunday School*

One failure of the young man teacher mentioned earlier was that he was not getting his pupils ready for the lesson. He simply assumed that because the lesson was interesting to him, it would be interesting to his pupils. For all his study, he was failing because he had neglected something basic in lesson preparation: looking at the content through the pupils' eyes, searching for common denominators between Bible passage and Junior living, seeking at every step in his study to see the real live pupils he taught, asking, "How can I get this lesson into the lives of my pupils?"

Now let's watch a teacher who understands the implications of this law.

Jane Forbes opened her new teacher's quarterly. "The five lessons of Unit I," she read, "will help the pupils find an answer to the question, How did we get our Bible?"

Now there was a project with some challenge! Eleven-year-olds like to know how things began.

Did that mean that Jane would have an easy time as she taught this unit? Did she need only to put the unit question before her pupils, then watch as they set to work with zest and enthusiasm to find out how we got our Bible?

Nothing could be more unlikely. Jane could count on her Juniors being interested on Sunday—but interested most probably in the world they lived in. To divert interest from outside subjects to "How we got our Bible" would require some strong competing interest.

Jane laid plans.

She bought a Hebrew language scroll and borrowed a Greek New Testament. In the church library she came on a real friend: an exhibit of large pages from the most famous of the Bible translations—pages from the Gutenberg, the Coverdale, the Vulgate, and other Bibles. From the American Bible Society she secured posters showing Bible verses in different languages. She secured some new translations of the Bible.

On arriving at Sunday school, the girls found these materials arranged attractively around the classroom. The large pages from the old Bible drew immediate attention.

"What are they?"

"Pages from your Bible." Jane led the girls to find corresponding pages in their own Bibles, to match the "queer" words with familiar ones.

"How long ago did the Bible look like this?"

Jane pointed to the poster showing the most ancient pages and explained that about four hundred years ago certain pages of the English Bible looked like that. While interest was still lively, she asked, "Can you find in this room a Bible very much like the first Bibles?" When they pointed to the scroll, Jane placed it beside her own new teacher's Bible. "Can you guess how long it took the Bible to grow from scrolls to books?" Jane wrote down the guesses. "Can you imagine what it cost to change the language you see in the scroll to the language in your Bible?" (More guesses.) "Do you know why the Bible had to go 'underground' for many years?"

Then Jane asked whether the girls would like to spend five Sundays finding the answers to these questions—in tracking the Bible back to its very beginning. The unit was launched on a note of adventure and pleasant anticipation.

But let us suppose that Jane had interrupted a discussion of a Saturday afternoon skating party with the demand, "Let's put all outside things out of our minds and get started. The subject we begin today is 'How we got our Bible.'"

Do you think the girls would have been "ready" for the project under those circumstances?

Some teachers can, by authority of their personalities, impose their will on the wills of the young—temporarily at any rate. Jane could probably have succeeded in getting her pupils (outwardly at least) to "be quiet" and "pay attention." But the true teacher is never satisfied to get attention by external pressure. He knows that the learning incentive should come from within the

learner, that his task is, somehow, someway, to get hold
of the inner springs of action, to help his pupils feel,
"I will learn this because it has point and meaning for
my life," not merely, "I will learn this because my teacher
wants me to."

3. Factors That Condition Readiness

There are many factors that condition a pupil's readiness to learn.

(1) *There is the factor of physical readiness.*—All of
us know how difficult it is to concentrate when physical
conditions are unfavorable—when the room is too hot or
too cold, when it is overcrowded or badly ventilated,
when the seat is too high or too hard, and bothersome
sights and sounds distract the mind.

Because unfavorable physical conditions can affect the
pupil's readiness for learning, the teacher will do what
he can to see that the environment works with him
rather than against him.

(2) *There is the factor of emotional readiness.*—When
a person is cross or out of sorts or angry or hurt, his
readiness for learning is blocked. Every teacher knows
"those Sundays" when the class is especially boisterous,
when tempers are short and the class is edgy. Sometimes
a relaxing activity—a map game, a quiz, a picture search,
a Bible drill—will work off excess spirits and establish a
better readiness for learning. Many teachers find that a
prayer at the beginning of the class period can prepare
the pupils emotionally for the lesson. But prayer should
not be used as an instrument of discipline. Opportunity
for praying should be given the Juniors every time the
teacher feels they can pray sincerely.

Sometimes a lesson fails to get interest simply because
it is over the heads of the Juniors, because it is slanted
more for Intermediates or Young People. For example,
a teacher of ten-year-old boys, in teaching the lesson on

Ruth, ignored the lesson's obvious values for Juniors—Ruth's loyalty, unselfishness, devotion to her mother-in-law—and emphasized the romance between Boaz and Ruth—an aspect to which the pupils were completely indifferent.

(3) *There is the factor of capacity.*—The pupil is not *ready* for teaching that is beyond his mental grasp. We would not try to teach a three-year-old to say the books of the Bible or explain to a four-year-old the principle of regeneration. Nor is a Junior ready for a unit of lessons on courtship and marriage.

When teachers try to force on Juniors something beyond their mental grasp, they are teaching, but, teaching something they do not intend to teach; the Juniors may be getting the feeling that the Bible is unreal or that it is not interesting.

II. THE LAW OF EFFECT (OR SATISFACTION)

Here is the way the textbooks state this law: When an activity is accompanied by feelings of pleasure or satisfaction, there is a tendency to repeat that activity until it is built into behavior and habit. Put the law negatively, and it highlights the same truth: When an activity is accompanied by feelings of distaste and unhappiness, there is a tendency to avoid that activity.

1. *How the Law Works*

Here again we observe a principle close to everyone's experience. Daily we come up against situations resulting from people working with or against that law. A mother is deeply distressed about her twelve-year-old daughter. The girl is unco-operative, takes no pleasure in "keeping the house nice," never volunteers to help with the cleaning, cooking, or sewing. "And when she does help," the mother complains, "she is slipshod and listless. I have to keep after her every step of the way to get the job done."

It would be a shock to that mother to learn that she herself is partly responsible—responsible because she fails to see that her daughter gets the satisfaction that comes from self-expression in the performance of her duties. The girl does her work to the accompaniment of countless orders and minute instructions. Every detail of every task is supervised. Tasks that could provide creative opportunity descend to the level of routine drudgery. The result of the girl's labors represents her *mother's* taste, her *mother's preferences*, never her own.

Another mother encouraged her daughter to put her best thinking into the household tasks she performed. She was allowed to arrange flowers, group furniture, plan meals, prepare desserts. Sometimes the girl turned out work that, compared to her mother's, left much to be desired. But the achievement of a piece of perfection was not the goal. The important thing, in the mother's thinking, was that her daughter should learn to enjoy homemaking, should find satisfaction and a sense of achievement in all she did.

2. *The Law at Work in Sunday School*

Sunday school teachers need to understand the importance of helping Juniors find satisfaction in their study of the lessons, in the churchgoing experience, in the learning of memory work.

(1) *In teaching the Bible lessons.*—If a teacher works to make the reading of the Bible in his classroom an interesting and thought-provoking time; if he sends his pupils to the Bible to find answers to problems that challenge their curiosity and command their best thinking; if he guides his pupils to see parallels between the lesson passage and their own everyday experiences; if, above all, he himself opens his Bible with anticipation

and relish, then Bible reading is going to be for the Juniors a vigorous and stimulating experience—one they will very probably want to repeat the next Sunday and the next.

The teacher in such a case has obeyed the law of satisfaction.

(2) *In motivating preaching attendance.*—If the teacher gets excited about the opportunities the preaching service offers Juniors for worshiping, learning, and growing; if he leads them to participate intelligently and creatively in the praying and singing and listening; if he directs their attention to the sermon by means of challenging questions, then the church experience will be pleasant and rewarding—one which the Juniors might be led to repeat until church attendance has become a habit.

One superintendent who feels that guiding Juniors to get satisfaction from the church service is an especial responsibility of Junior workers gives a sermon assignment each Sunday. "Our preacher is going to preach about some of you today," she might say one Sunday. "Let's see how many of you can find yourselves in the sermon on 'Six Kinds of Christians.'" Again she might say, "Our preacher is going to have a new reason for giving today—one I never thought of before. In church today you will find that reason." Or, "In church today you will learn the name of our preacher's favorite Bible character."

On the next Sunday she discusses what the Juniors found out from the sermon.

Again, this teacher will devote an entire assembly program to study of the church bulletin, helping Juniors to understand the meaning of such words as "invocation," "benediction," "invitation hymn," and so on.

Many teachers encourage their pupils to follow in their own Bibles the Scripture reading as the preacher reads.

Again they will give Juniors little booklets for recording certain important things about the sermon: the preacher's text and one good thought that helped them, for example; a story they liked, and so on.

Any preacher will be glad to give the Junior workers advance notice of his sermon content if he understands the purpose for which they want it—to help Juniors enjoy and benefit from his sermon.

(3) *In guiding the learning of memory work.*—In helping Juniors to memorize Bible passages and hymns, it is especially important that teachers understand and work in accord with the law of satisfaction. It is possible to blunt a pupil's appreciation for a Bible passage by the very way in which it is taught—by dull, monotonous drilling, lack of enthusiasm, absence of activity. On the other hand, it is possible to deepen appreciation of a passage by challenging activities.

Let us watch a teacher who understands the importance of using the principle of satisfaction in teaching the memory work.

The new memory passage for Juniors was Matthew 3:13-17, the baptism of Jesus. Their teacher introduced it in early time. She asked the two pupils who had been baptized to tell the others why they had done so. They decided it was to make an outside picture of what had taken place in their hearts. Then the teacher let those two Juniors describe their own baptism. "Whose example do we follow when we are baptized?" she asked next, and the answer was, "Jesus'."

The teacher then asked the Juniors to turn in their Bibles to the new memory passage to find if we truly follow Jesus' example. The pupils read the passage first just to get the details of the incident. Since some of the words and terms were far over the heads of ten-year-olds, the teacher had made a dictionary for the board. To the left she had written the hard-to-understand words and phrases; to the right she had written the simple words that they mean. For example, "Thus it becometh us to fulfill all righteousness" became "This is the right thing for me to do," and "suffered" she changed to the more familiar "let."

The teacher suggested that Juniors might memorize that passage in time to say in honor of all Juniors in the department who were baptized that quarter.

We no longer say to boys and girls, either directly or by our attitude, "You'll learn this and like it." Our approach is rather, "You'll like this—and learn it." That, in brief, is what we mean by the law of satisfaction.

3. Do Material Rewards Provide Lasting Satisfaction?

Sometimes teachers seek to provide satisfactions by the use of external rewards, by prizes and treats in payment for attending Sunday school, learning Bible passages, studying lessons, and so on. The trouble with such material motivations is that they do not get lasting results. When a child studies his lesson only to get a prize, his reason for studying is removed once the prize is won (or lost).

When we pay Juniors for living up to high ideals, we demonstrate that we ourselves have little faith in those ideals. The real reward, of course, is in the church-going experience itself, in the experience of worshiping, of drawing close to God, in learning from the minister ways to help the churchgoer live more wisely and happily, in singing and praying with others who love God. The reward for memorizing Bible passages is in having in the heart the great, wonderful words from God's Word that will help the learner throughout his life know the right thing to do.

If we ourselves have faith in the goals we set for boys and girls, if we work constantly to help them find satisfactions within the goals themselves, then we are building for something that will endure beyond childhood. (For further discussion of this subject see chapter 6.)

III. The Law of Exercise (Use and Disuse)

Here is the way the law is stated: An act once performed tends to be more easily performed again. Or, to put it another way, repeated responses to the same situation tend to make repetition easier, and failure to respond tends to make repetition less easy.

1. How the Law Works

We are all familiar with the working of this law. We know that the only way to learn to swim is to swim—to get down in the water and strike out for ourselves. Reading a manual on swimming and watching another swim—even the most expert swimmer—will never make a swimmer of you. You must exercise your own muscles, co-ordinate your own movements, *then practice the skill over and over until you have mastered it*. We learn to play the piano or type or drive an automobile in the same way.

Do the thing for yourself—and do it again and again—that, in plain words, is what this law means.

2. The Law at Work in Sunday School

To bring our illustration closer to the topic of this book, the only way a Junior will learn to find references in his Bible is to look up those references for himself—then repeat the act until he has acquired the skill of using his Bible. The only way he will learn to use the power of prayer is to turn to God in prayer at any time he needs his help.

(1) *In acquiring knowledge.*—Recently, in a church I attended, an evangelist addressed a group of boys and girls. He began his talk by asking them some very simple Bible questions. To the surprise of their minister and teachers, the boys and girls failed to answer some of the most elementary questions. What was wrong? Most of those boys and girls had been in Sunday school all their lives. Surely they had encountered those Bible facts at least once in their Sunday school experience.

The trouble probably lay in that very fact—that the Juniors had "encountered" the facts only. They had been exposed to some knowledge, but had not been given opportunity really to learn it, to make it their own. The fact that a Junior knows a Bible fact this Sunday is no guarantee that he will know it a month from now. Facts have a way of slipping out of the mind unless they are fixed by frequent recall. In Sunday school, if we want our Juniors to know and retain the truths we teach from Sunday to Sunday, we must make frequent use of recall.

Teachers should use the early time on Sunday morning for helping Juniors recall what they have learned in previous lessons. (See chapter 8 for detailed discussion of the early time.)

The teaching of the lessons offers many opportunities to recall what has gone before. The fact that our lessons are arranged in units gives them a relatedness that makes it natural to bring in truths from former lessons while teaching the current lesson. This practice also serves to strengthen and enrich the lesson being taught.

(2) *In guiding Juniors to better attitudes and conduct.* But of course the learning of facts is only the means to something higher and better. A Bible truth to be "learned" must be related to the experience of the learner, must be built into attitudes and behavior. There is a story of a Chinese boy who, when asked if he knew the Golden Rule, replied, "How can I know it? I have

not started behaving it." How right he was! And his answer is a clear illustration of what we mean when we speak of the law of exercise.

So, if teachers are to teach in order that Juniors may learn and retain what they learn, they must observe this law of exercise, not only in the learning of facts, but in the application of Bible truth to living.

Teachers must help their pupils see that the lessons they teach have some relation to everyday living; they must point out opportunities for Juniors to put the Bible truths they learn in their lessons into practice again and again—at home, on the playground, on the school bus, in the store. Teachers must encourage Juniors to relate their experiences on Sunday morning and then be ready to suggest further opportunities for living out the lessons. They must also watch for every opportunity that presents itself to help their pupils recall Bible facts.

IV. The Example of Jesus

Jesus, who knew more about human nature than anyone who ever lived, keyed his own teaching to the laws of learning. When he said to his disciples, "I have yet many things to say unto you, but ye cannot bear them now" (John 16:12), he was using the principle of readiness. He did not force his pupils to learn; he waited until they were ready for the more advanced lessons.

When he praised his disciples on their return from their first preaching tour, he was using the principle of satisfaction.

When he sent his disciples out to teach and to heal for themselves, he was using the principle of exercise.

LET'S THINK

1. As his Juniors came in a certain teacher gave each a "sealed order" (a small sealed envelope containing instructions). He asked them to keep them sealed until he gave his signal to read and obey. The orders were certain things to find in the Bible, on a map, out the window, in the lesson book, in a picture, and in a concordance. The teacher said, "Be ready to report on your assignment as we study our lesson." Which of the three laws of learning was that teacher observing?

2. A teacher worked hard to help her pupils find deep satisfactions from studying their Bibles. She guided them in interesting activities on the passages and opened up the meaning of words. She praised good work. She made the Bible reading activity enjoyable. Which of the laws of learning was that teacher observing?

3. A teacher worked on the principle of "never telling the pupils anything they could find out for themselves." He believed that pupils learn to do by doing. Which of the three laws of learning was he observing?

V

FACING YOUR TASK

A child, like a seed, develops from within, not from without. He develops according to God's laws of growth. A teacher can plant, a teacher can water, but it is God who gives the increase.

OUTLINE

I. WHAT IS TEACHING?

1. Is Teaching Explaining?
2. Teaching Involves Sharing
3. Teaching Results in Learning
4. Learning Is Changing
5. Getting a Definition

II. THE EXTENT OF PREPARATION

1. Preparation Means Self-improvement
2. Preparation Means Study of the Pupils
3. Preparation Means Study of the Bible

CHAPTER V

FACING YOUR TASK

I. WHAT IS TEACHING?

"I am going to teach Miss Brown's class this morning" a young woman said, then went into that class and spent the lesson period reading from a book of Bible stories. *Was she teaching?*

"I am going to teach the lesson on the resurrection this morning," a young man said, then spent his thirty-minute period delivering to the restless boys a carefully worked-out lecture on the post-resurrection appearances of Jesus. *Was he teaching?*

"I am going to teach the lesson on the first missionary journey," a woman said. But she used her lesson time to guide the girls in reading missionary verses from various parts of the Bible without giving them opportunity to discuss the ways *they* could be missionaries every day. *Was she teaching?*

"I taught a lesson this morning." How casually we say it! *How often can we really say it?* Before we answer that question, we must answer another one:

What do we mean by teaching?

1. *Is Teaching Explaining?*

It is hard, even for those people who understand what good teaching involves, to put together a definition of teaching that is both simple and adequate. I have heard many people try. "Teaching is explaining the lesson," some teachers have told me. Of course every teacher must do a certain amount of explaining, but we need do only a little recollecting to realize that explaining is not necessarily teaching. All of us have been exposed to some explaining at certain times in our lives—explaining that did not result in learning, or even in understanding.

When a person is explaining (or telling) we can be sure of one thing only: The explainer is active; his voice and his mind are at work. But that is no guarantee that the pupil's mind is also at work. Before a pupil can learn, something must stir inside of him, must reach out for the learning. As we found when we examined the law of exercise, we learn by the activity of *our* minds, *our* imaginations, *our* reasoning.

And until that has happened—until a pupil has learned —a teacher has not taught.

2. *Teaching Involves Sharing*

Something else is wrong with "explaining" as a definition of teaching. It leaves out the element of give-and-take between pupil and teacher, the quality of sharing so necessary in real teaching. The explaining teacher thinks of himself merely as a giver, of the pupil as a receiver. Actually each gives and each receives. The pupil shares his ideas, his wonderings, his questions—and through receipt of such confidences, the teacher learns where the pupil is and how far he needs to lead him.

The teacher shares his experience of Christ, his knowledge of the Bible, his feeling for his church, his riper wisdom, his more mature understandings.

Some students of the subject, aware of the importance of the sharing factor, have even suggested that we might define teaching as "sharing enthusiasms," or as "friendship with a purpose." Certainly in Sunday school, even more than in public school, the establishment of a friend-to-friend relationship is basic to good teaching.

3. *Teaching Results in Learning*

Since telling and explaining do not tell us what teaching is, we must look further. The dictionary offers,

"Teaching is causing another to learn." But that brings up another question: What do we mean by "learn"? What especially, do we have in mind when we say a pupil has "learned" his Sunday school lesson? That he has mastered some historical and geographical information? That he has memorized a Bible verse?

4. *Learning Is Changing*

No, as Sunday school teachers, we must expect more when we ask a pupil to "learn" his lesson. A Sunday school lesson is not learned until, as a result of its study, there has been some change in the pupil's heart and mind and life. What we are trying to do, first, is to help bring about the greatest change of all—the change that comes when we help boys and girls commit themselves to Jesus as Lord and Saviour. Then, when they have become Christians, we want to lead them in changing old attitudes, old ways of behaving until their lives more and more fit the ideals set forth by Jesus. In teaching every unit, every lesson, we should have as our purpose the guiding of changes in our Juniors, changes in knowledge, attitude, conduct or, to put it another way, changes in what the Juniors know, how they feel, and how they act (see chap. 6).

That is not to say that outstanding changes in attitudes and conduct will always be apparent after the teaching of one lesson or one unit, or even many units of lessons. A Sunday school teacher needs patience and faith in his ultimate goals—so much faith that he will keep on guiding Bible study, keep on leading his pupils to put Bible truth into practice, keep on helping them find deep and enduring satisfactions in right thinking, right behavior, even in the face of discouragements.

And little by little the pupils *will* change. It will not be a sudden or an even change. That is, the progress the Junior shows will not be a steady, uphill progress.

There will be good behavior, then a backset, then more improvement, then perhaps a reversion to old ways of behaving. But if we keep on teaching, praying, winning to Christ, it is almost certain that changes in the right directions will occur.

So learning must be changing. We cannot learn even one fact without being changed in some way—changed at least from a state of ignorance concerning that fact to a state of comprehension. If, through study of today's lesson, a pupil has learned the names of the first foreign missionaries, he has been changed in his knowledge. If he feels a real desire to be a missionary in his neighborhood just as truly as if he were in a foreign land, then he has acquired a change of attitude. If, as a result of this new attitude, he goes out and *does* something, brings a new boy or girl to Sunday school, for example, then he has been changed in conduct. (For a more detailed treatment of this subject, see chapter 6.)

5. Getting a Definition

We have decided, now, that there is no teaching without learning, and no learning without changing. We have agreed that the learner must do his own learning, and that sharing is an essential factor in teaching.

Putting all these ideas together, we might build a definition like this: *Teaching in the Sunday school is working with God to guide changes in boys and girls through shared experiences.*

Look at the word "guide." See how it puts the teacher in his proper place: on the outside of the learning operation. "Guiding" is all a teacher can do, all he dares try to do. He can no more force learning than a gardener can force development on the young and growing things in his care. All a teacher can do is to provide materials for learning, create a climate favorable for learning, seek to grow as a Christian himself, then with humility, reverence, and much patience watch over and pray over the growing.

A child, like a seed, develops from within, not from without. He develops according to God's laws of growth. A teacher can plant, a teacher can water, but it is God who gives the increase.

The word "experience" in the definition has significance, too. Some may ask, "But do the four walls of a Sunday school room allow opportunity for a Junior to have experiences?" Actually, to experience something means that we have had something happen in us or to us, something that we personally undergo. It means that we know something, feel something, desire something, do something.

The study of a picture may be an experience, for example, when it leads the Junior to have a feeling for the goodness and kindness of Jesus. The searching of a Bible passage may be an experience if it leads the Junior to put himself in the experience of Zacchaeus, for example, or the rich young ruler or the apostle Paul in prison. The discussion of an everyday problem such as honesty may be an experience if it leads the Junior to see that honesty means more than being straight in dealings with money.

"Teaching is working with God to guide changes that take place in boys and girls through shared experiences."

There is a statement big enough to cover the range and sweep of a teacher's task, limited enough to point the teacher to his proper place in the matter of learning, challenging enough to suggest the height and depth and breadth of his opportunity.

II. THE EXTENT OF PREPARATION

We all know that it is desirable to have a variety of good materials in the place where we teach on Sunday

—equipment, visual aids, all the tools that enrich and reinforce teaching. Actually, however, only three "materials" are absolutely essential. There must be someone to guide learning, someone to do the learning, and a subject matter to be taught. A teacher, a pupil, and a Bible—these are the three indispensables.

What does that fact have to do with lesson preparation? Just this—the teacher in preparing to teach, must concern himself with all three. He must study to improve himself, must study to improve his understanding of his *pupil*, must study to widen his own understanding and use of his *Bible* material.

1. Preparation Means Self-improvement

Since teaching implies sharing, every effort the teacher makes to improve the self he shares is a step in lesson preparation. We are not going too far when we say that when a teacher makes a right choice or fights an unchristian prejudice or builds a good habit into character, he is, in a way, preparing his lesson.

(1) *In the mental life.*—A teacher has an obligation, not only to grow in his spiritual life, but to stretch his mind, to be constantly pushing out the boundaries of his knowledge. "Thou shalt love the Lord thy God with all thy . . . mind." Why was God able to use Paul of Tarsus in so mighty a way? Because he had used his opportunities to get a good education, to discipline his mind, to acquire a wide understanding of the culture and affairs of his world.

A teacher should study. A teacher should read. A teacher should listen. A teacher should discuss.

Do we realize, too, that the Bible offers us our best chance to educate ourselves? "No man can be wholly uneducated who really knows the Bible," Jacob G. Schurman, a great American educator and diplomat, declared. "Nor can anyone be considered a truly educated man who is ignorant of it." And Robert A. Millikan, scientist and Nobel Prize winner, states, "I consider an intimate knowledge of the Bible an indispensable qualification of a well-educated man."

Even those teachers with little formal schooling can do much to improve their general education by utilizing their spare minutes and availing themselves of the books and magazines at hand.

(2) *In the spiritual life.*—Because souls as well as bodies starve without food, Christian teachers have to cultivate those practices that nourish the life of the spirit—Bible reading, praying, worshiping in the church services, soul-winning.

These practices, if they are genuine, will result in better Christian thinking and better Christian living. Our spirits are renewed and reinvigorated most of all by practicing our Christianity: winning souls to Christ, sharing with the needy, responding to human suffering with love and concern.

How much broader, then, is lesson preparation than the study of one lesson! We teach by all that we are. Preparation means constantly growing as a person, growing unto the measure of the stature of the fulness of Christ.

(3) *In the physical life.*—Boys and girls are especially responsive to personal attractiveness. I have seen them eyeing an attractive lady or a manly man at promotion time with an "I-hope-we-get-her" or "I-hope-we-get-him" look.

What is it composed of—this quality so easy to spot, so hard to analyze—attractiveness! A nice voice helps, and so do neatness, an open face, pleasant features, good physique.

But physical attractiveness depends on something more—something from within. Some of the teachers most loved by children are teachers who can lay no

claim to physical good looks. Children respond to a re-
laxed, secure personality—to a teacher who is emotionally dependable. Unevenness of temper—a mark of
immaturity in itself—is especially distasteful to children
who are immature themselves. They want their teachers
to be grown-up on the inside as well as the outside.

There is another common denominator among most
physically attractive people. They are outgoing rather
than withdrawn. They are interested in things outside
their own concerns, in people outside themselves. They
care about the world they live in and all its people.
That is a quality irresistibly appealing—one always re-
flected in the physical features.

So you see how hard it is to separate the physical
from the spiritual. When we try to analyze physical
attractiveness, we find that it leads right back to the
kind of person a teacher is—to the quality of his spiritual
life. What a teacher is shines through in his expression.
And it is by what they see that they decide about their
teacher—"She's nice," or "He's O. K."

2. *Preparation Means Study of the Pupils*

"I am not studying just to teach a lesson; I am studying
to teach Johnny." A teacher beginning the preparation
of his lesson must keep in mind that Johnny is as much a
part of his lesson as the Bible passage he is to teach. A
lesson is not a lesson until it has touched the heart and
life of a human being.

(1) *Using the class record book.*—The class record
book is a help to the teacher in remembering that he
teaches individuals as well as lessons. On that page
there is a "picture" of Johnny—a picture of what he has
done or failed to do in his Sunday school work. The
record book does not tell a teacher all he needs to know
about his pupils; it does nudge him into considering
some of their needs as he prepares.

But how may a teacher get to know what Johnny is like on Monday and Tuesday as well as on Sunday? We all know that a Sunday morning acquaintance is insufficient.

(2) *Listening to what Juniors say.*—A teacher may learn much about his pupils by listening to what they say in class and elsewhere. A recent book is entitled *Teacher, Listen, the Children Speak.* That is good advice for any teacher. Most of us who teach boys and girls are very much concerned with what we have to say to them, but attach little importance to what they are saying to us. Through the opinions our Juniors express, the questions they ask, the answers they give to our questions, Juniors are telling us things about themselves, telling us where they are mentally and spiritually—and it is only through knowing where they *are* that we may know how far they need to be led.

(3) *Visiting in the homes.*—A teacher can learn many things about a pupil by visiting in his home. Some things he cannot learn any other way. There he gets a picture of the type of living that has shaped the Junior he knows. He learns what the parents are like; he can tell something about the various relationships in the home—factors that influence the Junior's thinking and behaving. Children are what they are largely because of the people they live with—and the way those people live together. A teacher never truly knows a pupil until he knows the home from which he came.

(4) *Making other weekday contacts.*—But there are many things a teacher cannot learn just from visits. He needs to be with his pupils in natural situations. He needs to see how they play with other boys and girls, how they lose and win, how they adjust to a group.

That is why class meetings and class parties, picnics, and hikes are so valuable. As the teacher watches his pupils in their perfectly natural reactions, he can learn their many needs and problems.

(A more detailed treatment of the teacher's weekday opportunities for strengthening his teaching is given in chap. 9.)

3. *Preparation Means Study of the Bible*

But even when the teacher has worked to improve himself, even when he thoroughly knows his pupils, he is not yet ready to teach. He must be familiar with the guidebook of Christian living, the textbook of the Sunday school.

Preparation means study of the Bible. Relating that textbook to life is the Christian teacher's peculiar contribution through teaching in the Sunday school.

We have discussed the necessity of a teacher's widening his general Bible knowledge by regular study (chapter 2). We will discuss in chapter 7 the teacher's study of the Bible as the basis for the lessons he teaches.

LET'S THINK

1. Which of these statements do you think is the most adequate definition of teaching in the Sunday school?

(1) Teaching is explaining the lesson facts.

(2) Teaching is filling the pupil full of inspiration.

(3) Teaching is working with God to guide changes that take place in boys and girls.

(4) Teaching is imparting knowledge.

2. Name one objection to each of the other three as a definition of teaching.

3. If teaching is the sharing of knowledge and beliefs and attitudes, what responsibility does this place on the teacher?

4. What three opportunities are available to any teacher who wants to know more about his pupils?

A LESSON BEGINS WITH A PURPOSE

The starting point of any effective lesson is a goal in the teacher's mind—some sort of idea of the changes that might be brought about by his teaching.

OUTLINE

I. LESSON STUDY BEGINS WITH UNIT STUDY

   1. Defining a Unit

   2. Deciding on a Unit Purpose

II. WHAT A GOOD UNIT PURPOSE SHOULD SEEK TO ACCOMPLISH

   1. A Change in Knowledge

   2. A Change in Attitude

   3. A Change in Conduct

Chapter VI

A LESSON BEGINS WITH A PURPOSE

I. Lesson Study Begins with Unit Study

"How soon should a teacher begin studying next Sunday's Sunday school lesson?" Most of us, regardless, of our own study habits, will reply, "Sunday afternoon, or Monday at the latest," believing with that answer that we have set a fairly high standard of preparedness.

But is Monday, or even Sunday, soon enough? Teaching, we have already decided, is more than "bringing the lesson to the class." Teaching is trying, with God's help, to *do something* for Jerry Jones and Judy Brown—to bring about needed changes in their way of looking at things, feeling about things, doing things.

The starting point of any effective lesson is a goal in the teacher's mind—some sort of idea of the changes that might be brought about by his teaching.

But a teacher cannot wait until just before next Sunday's lesson to choose that goal. If he is to teach for big and worth-while changes, he must begin, at the time his new quarterly comes, to survey all the lessons of the quarter, to note their subject matter, the part of the Bible from which they are taken, the titles, pictures, memory passages—and especially the way the lessons are grouped into units.

The last eight words of that sentence are important. *The beginning of the study of any single lesson is the study of the unit to which that lesson belongs.*

1. Defining a Unit

We do not teach lessons—single, isolated lessons; we teach units of several lessons. In our Junior courses all

[75]

the lessons are arranged in groups or blocks of lessons called units. A unit may be defined as a group of lessons each of which contributes to the same general purposes. There may be three lessons in a unit—or four or five or even more.

The reason for grouping lessons into units is that teachers can realize larger purposes—work toward bigger changes—when they have several lessons to help them than when they have one lesson.

So we might answer the question with which this chapter opens by saying, "A teacher begins to study his lessons when he decides on the purpose for the whole unit of lessons he is to teach."

2. Deciding on a Unit Purpose

How does a teacher decide on the purpose he will work toward as he teaches the four or five or six lessons of a new unit?

As we think about that question, let us imagine that you have just received your new quarterly, and have opened it to discover what your new lessons will be about.

This is an important moment. You are beginning at this point to study next Sunday's lesson. The way you feel about this new venture is important.

(1) *Sense the challenge of the unit's possibilities.*—I remember reading somewhere, a long time ago, that the poet John Keats felt something of the same excitement on opening a new book that an explorer feels when he embarks on a voyage to far and unknown lands.

If a teacher embarks on the study of a new unit with a little of the explorer spirit, with the feeling that there are fresh and wonderful meanings to be discovered in the Bible passages he is about to teach, new vistas of understanding to be opened up, he has taken the first step in the preparation of interesting and effective lessons.

(2) *Survey the Bible passages.*—The natural thing to do first, on opening a new quarterly, is to notice what lessons you are to teach, to discover from which part of the Bible you will be teaching. Is this a New Testament or an Old Testament unit? Whose life will you be studying? How many passages are in narrative form? All of this is of interest to you who will be studying and teaching from these passages. Many teachers read all the Bible material of the unit before they begin teaching the first lesson of that unit.

(3) *Study the printed discussion of the unit.*—We may imagine that you have found that the first five lessons of the quarter are grouped together into a unit called "Learning to Be a Follower of Jesus." Always you will find, near the beginning of the teacher's quarterly, one or more pages which present a discussion of the first unit. There is usually a brief survey of its subject matter and a statement of the purposes which the lesson writer thinks are attainable. You will of course, want to study these printed purposes. Often you will find that they are suitable for your purposes, and you will get them in your mind as goals to work toward in teaching the unit.

(4) *Consider the needs of individual pupils.*—But as you study the printed purposes in your quarterly, you must see more than printed purposes. Beyond the printed page you will see the faces and the personalities of your Juniors. Aware of their special needs and capacities, you will ask yourself, "Do these purposes suggest actual changes that need to be brought about in the lives of Judy and Sue and Lynn and Betty?"

You will keep that question in mind as you scan the Bible passages for all the lessons. What do they hold in the way of special help for the special problems of your Juniors?

Sue is not a Christian, we will say. You note that the opening lesson is based on Jesus' call to the four fishermen. This lesson should help you work toward meeting Sue's greatest need—the need to make a personal decision for Jesus.

You see a lesson on the good Samaritan—and you think of Judy. There are influences in Judy's life that have caused her to form intolerant, overbearing attitudes toward people she considers "beneath her." Here is a chance to help Judy realize that to a follower of Jesus, everyone who needs his help—regardless of his class or station—is "my neighbor."

And Lynn is trying to live as a Christian in a family of foster parents who give her little or no encouragement. If she is a good follower of Jesus, it will be in spite of home influences rather than because of them. Will that lesson based on Peter's behavior on the night of the betrayal—the time when he followed Jesus afar off —help Lynn in her problem? Do you see what you are doing? You are preparing to teach, even though you have not yet concentrated on one particular lesson. You are taking a survey of your Bible material, and a survey of your pupils' needs to find all the places where the two might come together.

Not until you have done this, are you ready to answer the question, "As a result of five lessons on 'Learning to Be a Follower of Jesus,' what do I want to happen to my pupils?"

When you have decided on the answer, you have chosen your unit purposes.

II. What a Good Unit Purpose Should Seek to Accomplish

You will usually find that the lesson writer's suggested purpose for a unit will fit one or more of three types.

One type will usually be stated somewhat like this: "The purpose of this unit of lessons is to lead my pupils to know . . ." or, "to help my pupils become familiar with. . . ." That is a knowledge purpose.

Another type of purpose may be expressed something like this: "The purpose of this unit is to help my pupils feel a desire to . . ." or, "to help my pupils want to. . . ." This is an attitude purpose.

There may be a purpose that reads: "The purpose of this unit is to help our pupils form the habit of . . ." or, "to help my pupils grow in the ability to do. . . ." That is a conduct purpose.

The teacher should have as his purpose in teaching a unit the changing of the pupil's *knowing* or the changing of his *attitude* or *feeling* or the changing of his *doing* or his *conduct*. Whether or not the purposes printed in the quarterly are stated in this form, the teacher should so plan his own unit purpose.

This does not mean (as has already been pointed out) that there will be spectacular changes in attitudes and conduct on the part of the pupils at the end of a unit's study. Often there will be no visible changes at all. Sometimes there will be changes but changes the Sunday school teacher will never see. Sometimes the changes will be so gradual that not even those nearest the child will be able to detect them until years in the future.

A teacher is not to be discouraged if he does not see quick results in Christian living from his teaching. The steady, Sunday-by-Sunday searching of God's Word, the practicing of its teaching, the growing feeling of satisfaction and happiness in doing what it says—such basic procedures will eventually result in better living for our Christian Juniors.

1. *A Change in Knowledge*

We said above that one of the purposes of a unit

should be a change in the pupil's knowledge. As a result of the study of every unit and every lesson, the Junior should know something. The teacher should plan for his pupils to acquire some factual Bible knowledge: what happened, who said what, when it happened, what the incident meant.

In the unit on "Learning to Be a Follower of Jesus," you might decide that you want the Juniors: to know that the first step in becoming a follower is to accept Jesus as Saviour; to know that Jesus gave in the Sermon on the Mount a set of principles for followers, and to understand what these are; to know from the principal events in Jesus' life what he wants his followers to do.

You will notice that all those purposes are concerned with *facts*—things you want pupils to have in their heads.

(1) *Is Bible knowledge important?*—There has been a tendency in recent years to minimize the importance of factual knowledge in Sunday school teaching. "Why should we ground our pupils in *facts?*" some people have asked. "The important thing is for them to get the truth of the lesson—to have something in their hearts rather than in their heads. What we are working toward is a change in attitudes and conduct."

But that reasoning overlooks a basic truth: An accurate and intelligent grasp of Bible principles is the only safe basis for forming right attitudes and conduct—and principles are learned through facts. The fact that so many pupils in the Sunday school, even pupils who attend regularly, are hazy about what the Bible actually says, was highlighted recently when a teacher of Intermediate boys reported his experiment in guiding a discussion on "The Christian Way of Life." He said that the boys were incapable of carrying the discussion through for the simple reason that they had no grasp of the facts about their subject. None of them could recall the Beatitudes or state a principle from the Sermon on the Mount.

Perhaps we have put our finger here on one of the reasons why so many boys and girls, as they grow older, become unsure of their beliefs—weak in their convictions. They have no foundation on which to build convictions— no foundation of factual knowledge.

All of this underscores the point we are trying to make: It is important for teachers of Juniors to have a wholesome respect for knowledge—simple, elemental, bedrock Bible knowledge.

(2) *Helping pupils acquire Bible knowledge.*—This means that we must require more actual Bible study on the part of the pupils at home. A Junior cannot report that he has "studied his lesson" until he has studied it carefully in his lesson book. (He should also read the Bible references, in the Bible.) Then on Sunday morning the study of the Bible passage should be the heart of the lesson. Not only must the teacher guide the Juniors in reading the Bible in class, but in searching the passage to get at its true meanings. Teachers should test their pupils' knowledge from Sunday to Sunday—and at the end of units.

(3) *Bible knowledge a means to better living.*—But while we stress the necessity of our Juniors knowing what the Bible teaches, we are not to stop with their *knowing.* The acquisition of Bible knowledge is never an end in itself. It is a means toward an end—the changing of a viewpoint, the lifting of a vision, the doing of a deed.

Over and over the Bible itself affirms that truth. It never advocates learning Bible truth just for the sake of learning Bible truth—but for what the learning can do for the learner and through the learner for all mankind: "Thy word have I hid in mine heart, *that I might not sin against thee.*" "Desire the sincere milk of the word, *that ye may grow thereby.*" "All Scripture is given by inspiration of God, and is *profitable* for *doctrine,* for *reproof,* for *correction,* for *instruction in righteousness.*" "Thy word is a *lamp* unto my feet, and a *light* unto my path." "But these are written *that ye might believe* . . ."

We guide our Juniors in memorizing John 3:16, not in order to recite John 3:16, but that, through learning that verse, they might catch some glimpse of the reach and sweep of God's love—and accept the gift which love made him bestow. We teach the lesson on Zacchaeus, not that the Junior may learn merely that Zacchaeus owned up and paid back what he had stolen—but that they may learn through his story Jesus' ideals of honesty. We teach the lesson on Jesus' visit to the synagogue at Capernaum, not just to learn that it was Jesus' custom to attend the worship service on the sabbath, but that Juniors may follow Jesus' example in their own lives.

The teacher who thinks his lesson is "taught" on Sunday morning when his pupils can say back to him the names of the characters in the lesson, the places they visited, and the other facts of the lesson, has never caught the highest vision of the purposes of Sunday school teaching. He is teaching Bible *history* and Bible *geography*. He is not teaching a Bible lesson.

2. A Change in Attitude

When a teacher has decided what he wants his pupils to know as a result of the new unit, he has taken an important step toward the planning of his unit—but only *one step*. His next—and bigger—concern is, "How can I use these lessons to help my pupils in their living—what do I want them to do and what do I want them to feel?"

A Junior lesson should be taught for the purpose of helping Juniors feel something—a high desire, a want to do. When a teacher has decided what that desire or want shall be, he has chosen his attitude purpose.

Let's go back to the unit, "Learning to be a Follower of Jesus." Let us say that you have already decided what you want your pupils to know. Now you are ready to think about attitudes, what you want them to *feel*. You might decide that as your attitude purposes you want your pupils to feel a growing need of Jesus as Saviour, to believe that only by following him can anybody live happily and well, and to desire to be his follower and to live as nearly as possible as Jesus lived.

(1) *A distinctive of Christian teaching.*—When a teacher begins planning in terms of attitude, he is getting at the very heart of Bible teaching—he has touched one of the distinctives of Christian teaching.

Right conduct—if it is to be the sort of conduct that endures, the kind that grows into right habits of behavior —must have its roots in right desires, in worthy attitudes.

If Jesus taught anything at all, he taught that a changed life must begin with a changed heart. Good deeds always have their roots in good thinking. A wicked act—murder, Jesus cited as an example, or adultery—begins with nothing more than a feeling, a hidden inside thing no one can see—a wrong heart-condition! "A good man out of the good treasure of the heart bringeth forth good things: and an evil man out of the evil treasure bringeth forth evil things"—those are the words of Jesus. And again he said, "But those things which proceed out of the mouth come forth from the heart."

(2) *Attitudes determine conduct.*—When we seek to help our pupils form right habits of conduct without lifting their desires to the level of that behavior, we are beginning at the wrong end of the line. We are centering attention on deeds before we work on motives. We are concentrating on the outward act rather than the inner drives that lead to the act.

It is possible, for example, to get a Junior to attend church services Sunday after Sunday even though he feels no real desire to attend—or any satisfaction in the experience. He may be going because a parent has said he must go, or because a teacher has offered some tempting material reward or used a competitive activity.

That sort of motivation might get the behavior that parents and teachers desire—but will the behavior endure? Will it grow into right habits? It is always possible, when we use such external means, that the good conduct will cease when these outer controls are removed.

The teacher is much more apt to get Juniors to form the habit of church attendance that will endure if he works at the other end—with the Junior's inner desires.

He may do that by building up the Junior's interest in the church services, by helping him understand and appreciate what each part of the service means, by arousing interest in phases of the sermon, by challenging the Junior to find facts of interest in the sermon—then by engaging him in a stimulating discussion of the sermon. This principle relates closely to the law of satisfaction (see chapter 4).

(3) *Can attitudes be taught?*—When we hold up the example of Jesus to our Juniors; when we illustrate our lessons with incidents from the lives of men and women, of boys and girls who dared to do right; when we help our pupils think through life situations to discover whether right thinking and honorable conduct actually do lead to true happiness—then we are working in the realm of right attitudes. We are trying to help Juniors *want to do.*

The teacher should remember, too, that attitudes are *caught* as well as *taught.* The way the teacher himself *feels* about Jesus, God's Book, other people—all his own attitudes—communicate themselves to the pupils he teaches.

So in your unit planning, you will decide what you might reasonably expect your pupils to want to do. You will arrive at that decision by your own examination of the Bible passages and your study of the lesson writer's purposes.

3. A Change in Conduct

But there is not much use in working to arouse the pupils' desire to do if we give them no opportunity to translate desire into action—to be doers of the word and not hearers only.

In the unit on "Learning to Be a Follower of Jesus" your conduct purposes would be "to lead the Juniors to make a decision for Christ; to try every day to do what Jesus would want them to do."

(1) *Specific guidance is necessary.*—These purposes are necessarily abstract, but each lesson will suggest some concrete thing to do in order to reach the unit purpose. When, for example, after a study of Jesus' words in Matthew 25:34-40, the pupils feel a true desire to help a needy person, the teacher should be ready to suggest someone they might help and lead them to decide on a way to help. If, after a lesson on Peter's denial, the Juniors feel a real resolve in their hearts to witness for Jesus even when it is hard, the teacher may suggest that they learn a prayer verse to repeat in the morning and at night—and especially in moments of temptation. If after a lesson on Jesus' home in Nazareth, the Juniors decide that they can make their homes happier, the teacher might help them draw up a set of rules to keep in their rooms and check each day.

(2) *Juniors grow by doing.*—When we plan something for the pupils to do, we are obeying the law of exercise (see chapter 4). Juniors will never learn to be doers by merely hearing about others who performed Christian acts. They will not even learn by reading principles of

right living in the Bible—if they read them only. They learn by actually putting into practice themselves—over and over—the Christian principles found in God's Word.

LET'S THINK

1. Name at least one advantage in teaching in units rather than in teaching single, unrelated lessons.

2. When should a Sunday school teacher begin studying next Sunday's lesson?

3. Why is it not advisable for a teacher to adopt the lesson writer's purposes just as they are written? What important thing does a teacher know that no lesson writer knows?

4. How many of the following facts about a pupil would you need to know in order to help him through teaching a lesson on "Making My Home Happy"?

—The pupil is not a Christian.
—Father and Mother are not Christians.
—Pupil is the oldest of a large family.
—The home is very needy.
—Family includes an invalid grandmother.
—The mother works.

5. How would you answer a person who said, "Knowing Bible facts is not important. The important thing is to get the sense of the Bible passage."

VII

PREPARING THE LESSON

A Sunday school lesson is not just studied. It is grown. A good lesson needs at least seven days' growing time.

I. BEGIN STUDYING EARLY IN THE WEEK

1. Living with a Lesson
2. A Good Lesson Is Grown

II. READ THE BIBLE PASSAGE CAREFULLY, PRAYERFULLY

1. Feel Its Message
2. Get Personal Help
3. Find Help for the Pupils
4. See the Subject Matter Imaginatively

III. PROVIDE THE MATERIALS NECESSARY FOR ADEQUATE STUDY

1. The First Requirement Is a Bible
2. Study Both the Teacher's and the Pupil's Books
3. Use the Class Record Book in Your Lesson Planning
4. Study Pictures and Maps Along with the Lesson

IV. USE THE HELP FOUND IN SOURCE BOOKS

1. A Bible Commentary
2. A Bible Dictionary
3. A Concordance
4. A Harmony of the Gospels
5. A Topical Concordance

V. CHOOSE A LESSON PURPOSE, THEN STUDY TOWARD THAT PURPOSE

1. The Necessity for a Purpose
2. How to Choose a Lesson Purpose

VI. MAKE A WRITTEN LESSON PLAN

1. A Plan Aids in Informal Teaching
2. A Plan Conserves Ideas
3. A Plan Saves Time
4. A Plan Puts the Teacher's Stamp on the Lesson

Chapter VII

PREPARING THE LESSON

Let's imagine you have sat down to study next Sunday's lesson. You have had time, since you first examined this new unit, to decide what purposes you will try to reach as you teach its lessons, what you want your pupils to know, to feel, and to do.

But next Sunday is coming. Sometime this week you must sit down and concentrate on one lesson, not a group of lessons. The time, you have decided, is now.

So you settle down, ready to commence your study. What day of the week should this be? What will you do first?

No person can lay down to another person a set of hard-and-fast rules regarding the way he shall study. The way that is right and natural for me might not be at all right and natural for you. Some teachers like to begin by surveying the material in the teacher's book. Some read first the story in the pupil's book. The Bible passage, others insist, is the starting point.

While there is room for wide variation in ways of procedure, there are certain principles governing lesson preparation that do apply to every teacher studying every lesson. We are ready now to consider those principles.

I. Begin Studying Early in the Week

There is nothing new about that rule. Since grade school days we have known that "the earlier you get to studies the more time you have for studies."

1. *Living with a Lesson*

But what a Sunday school teacher needs is more than time to *study* a lesson. He needs time to *live* with that lesson. Eleventh-hour preparation on Saturday can get the lesson into the teacher. To get the teacher into the lesson, takes time—thinking time, musing time, pondering time, praying time, even sleeping time. For psychologists tell us that when the conscious mind is working on a problem or an idea, the subconscious mind gets busy, too; it is working even while our conscious minds are centered on something else—or while we sleep.

2. A Good Lesson Is Grown

A good Sunday school lesson is not just studied. It is grown. As a teacher turns the lesson over in his mind, reaching back into memory for personal experiences that will enrich it and out into life for true stories that will invigorate it, going back to the Bible for understanding that will illuminate it—that teacher is *growing* a lesson. He is doing something of the same kind of thing a gardener does when he cultivates and nurtures a plant.

A good Sunday school lesson needs at least seven days' growing time. A lesson can be ripening, maturing, as a teacher goes about his (or her) routine work, walking to the store, riding to work, waiting for a bus, sweeping, or washing dishes. We shall, of course, remember that this kind of preparing must be preceded by study of the Bible and by the careful choosing of purposes.

II. READ THE BIBLE PASSAGE CAREFULLY, PRAYERFULLY

You have come now to the heart of your lesson preparation. The Bible passage *is* the lesson, not just one phase of the lesson. We will discuss in this chapter many things connected with lesson preparation—pictures, source books, quarterlies, maps—but they are secondary. A Sunday school teacher has one textbook only, one course of study—God's Word.

Naturally, thorough study of the Bible passage is important. A teacher must know his subject matter, or he will have nothing to teach.

1. Feel Its Message

But for a Sunday school teacher something else is as important as knowing what the passage says. He needs to have a *feeling* about the passage. It is not enough to study to gets facts, to know what his textbook says; teachers of arithmetic or shorthand or geography do that. The Sunday school teacher needs to have *experiences* with the subject he teaches.

You have probably heard it said of a minister, "That man has a message." What does that mean? That what the man is preaching is so real, so vital to his experience, that he finds himself sharing something personal with his hearers—something that honestly matters to him.

We might bring the illustration closer home. When have you taught your best lessons? Think. Wasn't it when the subject you were teaching was something you personally had experienced—something you felt deeply about? You found yourself teaching then with sincerity and belief, and you found, too, that your pupils caught something of your own feeling about the subject.

A teacher, no less than a preacher, needs a message. Practices like those below will help make Bible study an *experience*, something the teacher can share.

2. Get Personal Help

It is a good idea for a teacher to read the Bible passage the first time to get something for himself. Study it first, not as a teacher searching for help for someone else, but as an individual, a seeking Christian. You will want to pray, first, that God will help you find in this passage some message that he has for you personally. Read the passage until you come to words that seem written especially for some need of yours. Mark those words.

You might choose one verse that you especially need as your verse for the day. Meditate on that verse, memorize it, make it the basis of your prayer that day.

3. Find Help for the Pupils

After you have read the Bible passage for yourself, you are ready to read it for your pupils. You are a teacher now, exploring your textbook with the sharp eye of one who is to guide others, probing into every verse, peering behind it, extracting from it every idea that suggests a way to meet some need of your pupils. You will want to mark verses that suggest help. You may even write by some lines the initials of a pupil who needs the help it suggests.

You will probably find as you search the passage in this way that you will get ideas for more needs than can be met by one lesson. Some of these ideas you will discard, but that will not matter. Your time has not been wasted. Your lesson will be richer for all the thinking and searching you did, even though some of the results are not used.

4. See the Subject Matter Imaginatively

There is still another suggestion for Bible study, one that is especially important for Junior teachers. Read your passage with imagination. Someone has said that every teacher of children needs the quality of "vicariousness," the ability, that is, to enter sympathetically into the experiences of another. Try to feel as the characters in this story must have felt: "Suppose I were in a prison in Rome waiting every day for the footstep of the executioner. How would I feel? What would I be doing? What would I be saying in the letters I wrote?"

Try to picture the setting of your passage. Get an understanding of the background. Read it to get a Junior's-eye view of its content.

The tools suggested below will aid you in seeing the story imaginatively—especially a commentary, a dictionary, maps, and pictures. Sometimes such a book as *The Bible Story Book* by Bethann Van Ness, for example, will provide the color and background necessary to fire the teacher's imagination.

III. Provide the Materials Necessary for Adequate Study

Even a good workman is crippled by poor tools—and if he has no tools, the work itself is stopped. The right tools can help a teacher in his planning, and the lack of tools can seriously handicap him.

1. *The First Requirement Is a Bible*

Every teacher needs a King James Version of the Bible. This is the Bible most familiar to most laymen. When you or I quote the Bible or even "think" the Bible, the words that come to our lips or into our minds are more than apt to be the beautiful words of the King James Version.

That will be your basic text, the Bible you will study from and use in class on Sunday. It is the version on which our Sunday school lessons are based. But it will be a fine thing if, in addition to this basic text, you own, or have access to, one or more newer translations of the Bible. The King James Bible was translated in 1611, and many of its words have gone out of our speech. Moreover, our very familiarity with its language sometimes dulls its meaning for us. We find our minds skimming over the surface instead of penetrating the inner truth of a passage.

But pick up a newer version and read next Sunday's lesson. See how its plain, vigorous speech jolts your mind into a keener understanding of this passage's meaning. If your pupils are mature enough, they, too, will find comparing the old with the new a stimulating experience. There are a number of good translations: The American Standard Version; the Revised Standard Version; Testaments translated by Helen Barrett Montgomery, Richard Francis Weymouth, Charles B. Williams, and J. B. Phillips; *The New English Bible* (New Testament); the entire Bible translated by James Moffatt; and one edition by Powis Smith and Edgar J. Goodspeed.

2. *Study Both the Teacher's and the Pupil's Books*

It seems almost unnecessary to state a fact so obvious. Yet there are churches that economize by providing only pupils' books for their teachers. While any teacher is handicapped without a teacher's book, denial of this aid puts a special burden upon the new teacher. It deprives him of so much that would help to orient him into his new work—the lesson writer's explanation of the purposes of each lesson, his interpretation of the Bible material, and, most of all, the suggested activities for Sunday morning.

On the other hand, there are teachers who ignore the study of the pupil's book in their preparation. The teacher should do just what he requires his pupils to do—read all the text in the pupil's book and do the required written work.

3. *Use the Class Record Book in Your Lesson Planning*

We have already said that the class record book, marked from Sunday to Sunday, is a picture of each pupil's achievements on the Six Point Record System for a year. In addition, if the teacher has filled in the information called for under each pupil's name in the book, he has a picture of the home background and other personal information that will suggest interests, needs, and problems.

The class book, open before the teacher during study

time, is a constant reminder to him to fit his Bible material to the size of his pupils, to "Juniorize" his lesson.

4. Study Pictures and Maps Along with the Lesson

Visual aids are not just extras to embellish a lesson. Rightly used, they are materials for strengthening teaching. If they serve that purpose, they must be studied at the time the lesson is studied. It is not enough just to show these aids to the pupils. The teacher must plan for activities that enrich them—and these activities must be related to the lesson. Maps and pictures must be before the teacher, then, as he studies as a part of his tool-kit equipment.

IV. USE THE HELP FOUND IN SOURCE BOOKS

1. A Bible Commentary

As its name suggests, a commentary is a volume devoted to comments on, or explanations of, the Bible passages. A teacher who is hungry to extend his Bible knowledge, to explore his subject beyond the limits of the background helps in the teacher's quarterly will find a commentary a valuable aid in his lesson study and an illuminating companion in his devotional reading of the Bible. Some commentaries are available in sets with one volume devoted to one or more books of the Bible. Then there are commentaries that treat the entire Bible within the space of a single volume. For the average Sunday school teacher, the latter type is adequate.

2. A Bible Dictionary

How did the town of Caesarea Philippi get its name? What is frankincense and what is myrrh? How much is a talent of money? How long is a cubit or a furlong? What is a centurion? What do you mean by a "sabbath day's journey"? If you have ever wondered about any unfamiliar word or term in the Bible, then a Bible dictionary is the volume you need. Like a regular dictionary, it gives definitions of words and terms, but it does more: it gives the reader a background of history and geography that will enable him to understand better the Bible passages he teaches.

3. A Concordance

Have you ever thought of a verse that would be the very one to enrich next Sunday's lesson—if only you could recall exactly what it said or where it was in the Bible? A concordance is the solution to that problem. A concordance lists alphabetically the principal words of the Bible and cites the passages in which they occur. With the aid of a concordance it is possible for a teacher to find any verse in the Bible if he can recall one or two principal words in that verse.

4. A Harmony of the Gospels

Which incident came first—the calling of the four fishermen by the Sea of Galilee or the meeting of Jesus with James and John by the Jordan River? The fact that one Gospel writer may contribute an incident in Jesus' life not mentioned by the others raises the problem of where to place those incidents in the chronological history of his life.

A harmony of the Gospels lists in parallel columns on each page each evangelist's account of the same incident. It also carries a chronological outline of all the events in Jesus' life.

5. A Topical Concordance

Imagine that you are teaching a lesson on prayer. You would like to enrich it with some of the great prayers of the Bible. A concordance will not help you, for its references are grouped by words, not by ideas. What you need is a topical concordance. In such a volume all the verses relating to a certain theme are grouped together.

V. Choose a Lesson Purpose, then Study Toward That Purpose

A young theological student had written his first sermon and submitted it to an older preacher friend for his criticism. He waited while the friend read it through, then asked doubtfully, "Sir, will it do?"

The veteran preacher looked at him steadily, and answered, "Will it do—what?"

A teacher, as well as a preacher, should be motivated in his preparation by the question, "Will it do—what?" The answer to that question—what he hopes the lesson will *do*—will be his lesson purposes.

1. *The Necessity for a Purpose*

You cannot plan your lesson constructively until you have at least sketched out your purpose. It determines everything you do. To begin planning what you will do and say without knowing what you expect to accomplish through doing and saying those things is to plan—and to teach—haphazardly. There is just one name for a lesson without an aim: an aimless lesson.

For the lesson, *as for the unit,* choose a purpose that answers the question: What do I want my pupils to know, to feel, to do? (See chap. 6.)

2. *How to Choose a Lesson Purpose*

After searching the Bible material, with your pupils' needs in mind, you will have several ideas for the direction your lesson might take. Then you consult your unit purpose to see how many of those ideas will contribute to the larger purpose for the unit. You will probably want to retain only those ideas that do relate to the unit.

Lesson purposes are much more concrete than unit purposes. A lesson purpose should be the statement of something that can be achieved through the teaching of one lesson. The unit purpose is usually too large to be attained in one lesson.

For example, a unit purpose might read, "To lead the Juniors to grow in the ability to follow Jesus in their everyday living." Your own purpose for one of the lessons in that unit might read, "To lead my pupils to know that being kind to those who wrong them is one mark of a Christian."

Many, many times, of course, the teacher will use the purposes suggested by the lesson writer, and certainly he will always want to study those statements. But there is one thing no lesson writer knows: the particular capacities and needs and interests of your own group of Juniors.

VI. Make a Written Lesson Plan

Why is it that so many teachers are overawed by the term "lesson plan"? If the term seems too scholarly for a layman like you, call it something else. Call it an outline, or your teaching notes. The important thing is to plan your lesson—and to put your planning into writing.

In *Principles of Teaching for Christian Teachers*, C. B. Eavey says, "While lesson plans may not be very important, planned lessons are supremely so. Anything that is not planned is planless, and anything that is planless will likely fail to accompish its purpose."[1]

Having a plan written down does not mean that you will have to follow that plan slavishly. Every teacher of Juniors knows that he cannot always proceed on Sunday

---

[1] C. B. Eavey, *Principles of Teaching for Christian Teachers* (Grand Rapids: Zondervan Publishing Company, 1940). Used by permission.

morning exactly as he had anticipated, that he must sometimes adapt his procedure to meet a need he could not know about until Sunday morning. That is good teaching. That is putting pupil needs above teacher-made plans. Juniors were not made for plans, but plans were made for Juniors.

1. *A Plan Aids in Informal Teaching*

Having a written lesson plan will help rather than hinder you in following the lead of your pupils. Writing down what you hope to do means that you must think yourself into the situation of Sunday morning, try to anticipate what will happen, then set down activities directed toward meeting actual purposes. That kind of preparation is a good background for whatever happens on Sunday morning. The thinking and organizing you have done around the lesson will show through in your procedure, even if the discussion moves on to another area.

2. *A Plan Conserves Ideas*

There are other reasons for writing down your plans. It is a way to conserve your ideas. Not many of us have memories so reliable that they can be trusted to retain a whole lesson procedure. Some of your best ideas may escape if you do not commit them to writing.

3. *A Plan Saves Time*

Writing down your plan saves Sunday morning time. When you organize your activities in an orderly way, you can tell if you have allotted an undue amount of time to some phase of the lesson and have slighted a more important part.

Writing a plan means that your lesson will be well-rounded. It will remind you to include the important things, the Bible reading, memory work, real-life activities, and so on.

4. *A Plan Puts the Teacher's Stamp on the Lesson*

Most important, writing down the plan makes the lesson *yours*. Even if most of the ideas you put on your plan sheet come from the quarterly, the fact that you have selected the activities, organized them in your own way, and written them down in your own handwriting means that now the lesson has in it something of you.

The teacher who does not write his own plan is liable to be a "quarterly teacher," depending on the quarterly for his lesson and referring to it in his teaching. The objection to this is that the teacher is so obviously teaching someone else's lesson. He is never thoroughly at home. His teaching lacks the conviction and sincerity that mark a lesson into which the teacher puts something of himself.

What should you put on your lesson plan sheet? At the top should go your lesson purposes, and under that a record of the activities through which you hope to realize those purposes. The activities should be in terms of what the pupils will do rather than what the teacher will do.

Here is a suggested lesson plan. Notice the different points under the heading, "activities." In the next chapter we will follow in imagination as a teacher uses this plan as the basis of his procedure on Sunday morning.

GUIDE SHEET FOR LESSON PLAN

Name of Unit_____Purpose of Unit_____

_____

Name of Lesson_____Purpose of Lesson_____

_____

Scriptures to Use_____

ACTIVITIES

(Under each point list one or more activities)

1. Provide Interesting Work for Juniors as They Arrive
2. Interest Pupils in the Lesson
3. Use the Bible Purposefully
4. Use Memory Verses
5. Use Memory Work
6. Use Pictures, Map, or Chalkboard (or all)
7. Relate the Lesson to Junior Living
8. Give Juniors Something to Do During the Week

LET'S THINK

1. Name two reasons why a teacher should start studying his lesson early in the week.

2. One of the following is a unit purpose, and one is a lesson purpose. Indicate which is which.

> To lead the Juniors to grow in willingness
> to share the gospel with others.
> To lead each Junior to decide to find and
> invite another to Sunday school this week.

3. Name one advantage in a teacher's reading the Bible passage devotionally in order to find help for himself before he begins studying the lesson.

4. Name three advantages in a teacher's writing down his own lesson plan.

ON SUNDAY MORNING

The time has come when your lesson plan will meet the test of Junior response. Conscious of the limits of your time and the limitlessness of your opportunity you wonder, "How can I make these Sunday school minutes count for most?"

Outline

I. Provide for Juniors as They Arrive
1. Review Previous Lessons
2. Get Ready for the Lesson
3. Work on Unit Projects
4. Learn Bible Skills
5. Arouse Interest in Memory Passages
6. Win to Christ

II. Use a Good Beginning to Get Interest
1. Will It Get Interest?
2. Does It Touch Junior Life?
3. Will It Lead to the Bible Lesson?

III. Use the Bible Purposefully
1. Give Juniors a Motive for Opening Their Bibles
2. Be Sure That Unfamiliar Words and Ideas Are Understood
3. Vary Bible Study with Interesting Activities
4. Put Bible Reading Early in the Lesson

IV. Use Memory Verses

V. Use Memory Work
1. Why Teach It?
2. When Teach It?
3. How Teach It?
4. The First Principle

VI. Use Visual Helps
1. Pictures
2. Maps
3. Chalkboards

VII. Get the Lesson into Living

VIII. Give Juniors Something to Do During the Week

Chapter VIII

ON SUNDAY MORNING

It is nine o'clock on Sunday morning. The time has come when the plans you have prayed over and studied over will meet the test of Junior response. Are those plans practical? Can they be used to change the thinking and the doing of any pupil in your class? Will this be the day when Jerry will realize that "God so loved me," and give his heart to Jesus? Will Henry sense the unworthiness of an old prejudice, and Fred catch a new vision of his responsibility as a follower?

Conscious of the limits of your time and the limitlessness of your opportunity, you wonder, How can I make these Sunday school minutes count for most?

This chapter is written to answer that question.

I. Provide for Juniors as They Arrive

In every Sunday school there are Juniors who arrive before starting time. Teachers who want to stretch their too-brief lesson period will look on that as a happy circumstance—an opportunity to add to their precious stockpile of teaching minutes.

The early teacher profits in other ways. As he talks with the pupils individually or in twos or threes, he draws a little closer to their experiences, their interests. By keeping the Juniors active and interested from the minute they arrive he may build up readiness for the lesson and forestall problem behavior. For problem behavior so often grows out of nothing more than boredom —and boredom out of inactivity.

On arriving at Sunday school the early Juniors should go immediately to their teacher. Even if assembly comes first (which is not the best plan), the early time should find teacher and Juniors working and studying together.

"But," some teachers ask, "what can you do when the pupils are coming in one by one? You can't start teaching until everybody is there." And "How can you have activities when you have to sit out in assembly?" We will try to focus on those early-time activities that are possible in any situation.

1. Review Previous Lessons

We have already seen that if a Junior is to retain what he has learned, he must have frequent opportunity to recall what he has learned. The early minutes provide a good opportunity to guide pupils in looking back at what was covered last Sunday, in reporting on assignments made then, in testing their understanding of the truths of the unit, in sounding them out on facts discovered in the quarter.

But, you may be thinking, can you hold a lively Junior's interest in a review, in just answering questions? Yes, if the teacher puts these reviews in attractive form, if he himself feels enthusiasm for, and enjoyment in, the quiztime. That's infectious!

Juniors enjoy, for example, a question box or an "ask-it basket." Each arriving Junior draws from the box or basket a slip bearing a question, and if he can answer the question, he keeps the slip. Of course the Junior will want to acquire as many slips as possible.

Or the teacher may write a few questions on the board, then give the Juniors sheets of paper bearing a row of numbers corresponding to the questions. They will write answers opposite the correct number.

Some teachers may type or pencil (using carbon paper) multiple copies of brief quizzes. Because Juniors do not have the writing or spelling ability to write long answers, it is a good idea to phrase questions that can be answered with a check or one word, or arranged so that Juniors may match an answer to a question by lines or numbers. It would be better, for example, to state, "Paul was born in Damascus ——Tarsus——Jerusalem——" than to ask, "In what town was Paul born?"

Maps and lesson pictures afford interesting methods of testing Juniors' recall of events and places. The teacher may state a certain happening, then let Juniors point to the place on the map where it happened (or mark it with a sticker). Or he may state a truth learned by one character in the unit, and let the Junior find the character in one of the pictures.

2. Get Ready for the Lesson

The teacher may use the early time for activities that build up readiness for the lesson or enrich its meaning. Sometimes each arriving Junior may be given an assignment which he must prepare and report on at some point in the lesson. The assignment may be to find something in the Bible, on a map, in a picture, in a harmony of the Gospels, concordance, or Bible dictionary.

The early time might be used in looking up unfamiliar words in a Bible dictionary, or in checking the lesson passage in a harmony.

Sometimes the thought questions in the quarterly may be completed in preparation for later discussion. Or each Junior might be given a life problem to think through, so that he may do better thinking about ways to apply the lesson to life.

Once in teaching a lesson on "Sharing What We Have," I asked each Junior in the early time to make an "inventory sheet" listing all the possessions she valued the most. Later these lists helped me to bring the lesson truth into the sphere of Juniors' living. Using the memory verse, we checked each treasure to see whether it could be ruined by moth, by rust, or stolen. Then we checked to see how many we could keep on and on in the only way possible to keep possessions—by using them to help others or give them happiness in God's name.

3. Work on Unit Projects

Sometimes the unit calls for an activity that will last for several lessons, for example, a Bible exhibit, a missionary corner, a service project such as sending pictures to a missionary, the preparation of a poster or notebook. Early time is a splendid opportunity to arouse interest in these projects, to plan for them, make reports, and in some cases, to do the actual work.

4. Learn Bible Skills

There is one Bible responsibility that belongs to the Junior teacher in a special way: helping Juniors learn the names and groupings of the books of the Bible. While this is something that should be learned when Juniors first come into the Junior group, teachers of older Juniors often find that they must make up for the oversight of a teacher of nine-year-olds and see that the skill is mastered. The early time is a good time for giving help in this learning.

Parrotlike drilling is not the most interesting way to learn the books of the Bible. It is much better to use some creative device such as a Bible bookcase. The Juniors practice putting into the bookcase little blocks of wood painted and lettered to resemble books of the Bible. Or the teacher may prepare colored bookmarks of stiff paper with the name of a Bible book across the end of each and guide the Juniors in placing each at the right book in the Bible.

It is also important that Juniors have practice in finding references in the Bible while they are learning the order in which books come. They must use the learning in the way it will be used later if it is to be a practical activity.

5. *Arouse Interest in Memory Passages*

Enriching memory work and motivating its learning is a good use of early time. On the day when it is introduced, the teacher may have on hand pictures that illustrate the various verses, and guide Juniors in matching verses to pictures. Juniors may be led to read the passage to feel its beauty and meaning. They may think through the meaning of unfamiliar words and ideas.

Reports on the learning of memory work may be made and good work recognized in the early time.

6. *Win to Christ*

Frequently the teacher finds himself alone with an early pupil for some time. If that Junior is not a Christian, this might be a precious opportunity to win him to Christ. In the quiet of this time it is natural to say: "Jean, I have been thinking of you and praying for you. I want you to know my Saviour." Or, "Betty, I believe you are a Christian. Would you like to talk to me about it?"

II. Use a Good Beginning to Get Interest

Lesson time! Everything that has gone before, early activities, the prayer with which you began this period, all lead up to the time when you introduce Juniors to the Bible lesson for today.

Now how are you going to introduce it? Will you ask your pupils to open their Bibles and read the lesson passage? Will you invite them immediately to get into a discussion of the Bible story?

You are going to do both those things—but not at the beginning. Your problem as you start the lesson is to build up readiness for the study, get minds to working, fire the pupils' enthusiasm for the lesson.

So you cast about for a good lesson opener or interest getter. It might be a thought-provoking question. It might be a problem close to Junior life. It might be a brief story which you begin and which the Juniors complete. It might be a picture. You are trying here to build a bridge over which the pupils will pass from their immediate concerns and self-interests to interest in the lesson before them.

Whatever beginning you choose, it must meet certain tests:

1. *Will It Get Interest?*

Unless you get interest, you might as well not teach; you cannot have a lesson. Before a pupil learns, you remember (see chapter 4) he must make some interested response to the learning. He must be ready for the learning.

A question is perhaps the best way to challenge interest. Even though you begin with a picture or a story, you will find that, in order to stimulate the pupils' thinking, you must ask some pertinent question.

The question should be carefully phrased. Do not ask questions whose answers are too obvious. You are not likely to get interest with, "Should a person be baptized before or after he is saved?" The answer is too obvious to demand thought. But the question, "If our legislature passed a law tomorrow that everybody in our state must be baptized, would that be a bad or good law?" is almost sure to excite interest.

In beginning the lesson on the test Jesus gave the rich young ruler, you would not say, "Are we called on to pass tests today just as surely as did people in the Bible?" A much better idea would be, "Do you take more tests in school—or out of school?"

Usually questions that can be answered with yes or no deaden rather than provoke thought. In a lesson on Christian citizenship it would be far better to ask, "How old do you have to be to become a citizen?" than "Can you help your country right now just as truly as when you are grown?"

2. Does It Touch Junior Life?

Usually it is better to begin with some interest of the Juniors than to begin with a question on the Bible material. At the start of the lesson Juniors are usually more concerned with their own interests than with the lesson. We must begin where the pupil is and lead him where we want him to go: into the Bible lesson.

It will help you remember this principle if you will try to use "you" in your opening rather than "they" or "people." You would not get as much response with the question, "Why do people give presents?" as with "Why did you give your mother a gift on Mother's Day?" You would not ask, "Does God answer people's prayers?" but "Does God answer every prayer you make?" (This last example may sound like a yes or no question, but it invites thought: God does answer every prayer—sometimes with yes, sometimes with no, and sometimes with "wait.")

A teacher will find that in addition to getting interest more quickly, the "you" beginning, the one slanted toward the Junior's living, will help him keep his entire lesson closer to Junior living.

3. Will It Lead to the Bible Lesson?

There are questions—interesting, stimulating questions —that will challenge attention, but will not get anywhere. They get the teacher into dead-end lanes or attractive by-paths. A good beginning will be one that will lead you into the lesson by the most direct path.

III. USE THE BIBLE PURPOSEFULLY

The study of the Bible passage is the heart of the lesson. Junior boys and girls, unlike younger pupils, use the Bible constantly in their study of the lesson. It is the part of the lesson they enjoy most, and a teacher should work to make it meaningful and fruitful.

Notice the word "use" in the heading. "Use" implies that Juniors are to do more than "read" the Bible. "Reading" may be a passive activity. In their Bible study Juniors search, hunt, check, compare, watch, ask, interview, follow. Even in Bible study Juniors need a variety of activities.

Here are some principles for making Bible study challenging in the class.

1. *Give Juniors a Motive for Opening Their Bibles*

It is not enough to say, "Let's open our Bibles now and read today's lesson." That motive is not strong enough to whet Juniors' appetites.

But suppose as you teach a lesson on "Peter's Right Answer" (Matt. 16:13-18), you guide a discussion of tests in schools, then suggest, "Let's open our Bibles to find the questions Jesus asked his pupils on their examination." Or, in teaching a lesson on Mary's love gift, "Let's open our Bibles to count how many ways a woman found to show love for Jesus." Or, in teaching a lesson based on Psalm 103, "Let's see how many blessings named in this passage are your blessings, too." Now there are some worthy motives for studying a Bible passage.

There is yet another reason for giving Juniors a good motive for opening their Bibles. When Juniors are reading to find something, they are applying their minds to the meaning of the passage; they must, if they carry out the assignment, concentrate on what it says.

Sometimes in an older Junior class it is a good idea to give individual assignments. Different pupils will be asked to look for different things. If we were teaching a lesson on Paul's letter from a Roman prison (2 Tim.

4:6-13), we might ask one pupil to watch for words that say Paul was not afraid to die; another, to notice words that suggest Paul might be planning to write more letters; another, if Paul might have been cold in prison; and another, the name of a loyal friend who stuck by Paul.

2. Be Sure That Unfamiliar Words and Ideas Are Understood

It is quite likely that some of the words in the passage you teach this morning, some of its expressions and terms, will be over the heads of your Juniors. Whenever that is true, it means that the teacher has another obligation: translating the hard, unfamiliar words into words that mean something to Juniors.

That is one reason why it is so helpful to study with a Bible dictionary and a Junior dictionary at hand. Neither of these, however, is a substitute for the teacher's own firsthand knowledge of the way Juniors talk and the experiences common to them.

(1) *A chalkboard dictionary.*—Before pupils arrive, the teacher may prepare a dictionary for the board. On one side of the chalkboard he will put each word he finds in the passage that is beyond a Junior's understanding. Opposite each of these words he will write its Junior synonym as in the "Word Explainer" or "Bible Translator" in the pupil's book. Before studying the passage, the pupils will read the words in the "dictionary," thus getting a basis for understanding its meaning.

(2) *Word tests.*—Another good word test activity is an "I find" quiz. If the lesson is the story of Jesus and Zacchaeus (Luke 19:1-10), for example, the teacher might say, "I see words that mean Zacchaeus was a prominent tax collector" (v. 2); "I see a word that means 'large crowd'" (v. 3); "I see words that say Zacchaeus was

little" (v. 3); "I see words that mean 'dishonesty'" (v. 8, "by false accusation").

3. *Vary Bible Study with Interesting Activities*

Any Bible passage chosen for a Junior lesson offers a rich variety of interesting activities. The pupils may pretend to interview a Bible character; they may divide into groups to study sections of the passage, then share their findings; they may go on an imaginary journey, or play out part of the story; they may pretend to be reporters and find incidents that they would want to put in the paper—if there had been papers in Bible times.

Make an adventure of Bible study: "Will half of you boys follow Gideon's men up the dark hillside? You will use your *eyes* to *see* something that happens. The rest of you will be sleeping in the enemy's camp. You will use your *ears* to *hear* something that happens." Or again, in teaching the lesson on the building of Solomon's Temple, you might suggest that the class climb Mount Zion and "take pictures" of the construction work. Divide class groups in half. Suggest that half take pictures of the inside of the Temple (they will read silently references covering the details of the interior), and that the other half stay on the outside and take pictures of the outside (they will read references that describe the outside).

These suggestions only hint at the vast variety of fascinating activities for conducting the Bible reading.

4. *Put Bible Reading Early in the Lesson*

It is a good idea to put study of the Bible passage early in the lesson. If you put your life discussion first and wait until the end of the lesson for your Bible reading, you are building a lesson without a foundation. Moreover, your Juniors will be too restless, by the time they get to it, to give the Bible study their best attention. Often, too, you will find that the lesson period is over before you have time to finish the Bible passage.

IV. USE MEMORY VERSES

Each memory verse is to the lesson what the text is to the preacher's sermon. It is its central truth, condensed, stripped down to its essence, summarized in a single verse. The purpose of a memory verse is to strengthen the teaching of the lesson, to clinch its core-truth. It should therefore be *used*, not just "recited."

You would not say, for example, "Now let's see how many know this memory verse," but, "Let's find in this memory verse something Zacchaeus discovered the day Jesus visited in his home." Or, "Let's see whether this memory verse would have made a good motto for Abraham to live by. Let's say it to decide why."

The truth of a memory verse can so often be used as a resolution or a wish or a prayer or a motto that the person or persons in the lesson might have made or prayed or lived by. When we use it like that, we lift the memory verse out of a page and set it down in life. We make it an experience that someone lived or might have lived rather than mere words to be learned.

A memory verse can be used in helping pupils apply the lesson to everyday living. Sometimes a teacher may have Juniors use a memory verse as a measuring stick to measure certain present-day Juniors. Or he may give life problems and let Juniors tell how these boys and girls in the stories would solve their problems if they lived by the memory verse.

V. USE MEMORY WORK

By memory work we mean the Bible passage or verses the Juniors are asked to memorize along with a unit of lessons they study. Memory work is a regular part of the course of study prepared for Juniors, and should be considered just as important as the lessons.

1. *Why Teach It?*

Why is it important that Juniors memorize so many passages of Scripture while they are Juniors? The answer lies in the last three words of that sentence. Because they *are* Juniors! Because they are boys and girls—and growing. What a child takes into his mind and heart during growing years gets into the structure of his thinking, his understanding, his outlook, while that structure is in the growing stage. It helps to form the basis of his beliefs and ideals.

A child who grows up ignorant of the great treasure passages of the Bible is a deprived child, and his mind and spirit will be the poorer all his life for that childhood deficiency.

2. *When Teach It?*

But memory work does present a problem. Should we use the Sunday morning time to teach it? The answer depends on what you mean by "teaching the memory work." There is certainly no time on Sunday morning to go over and over the words with individual pupils until those words can be repeated. Study of these passages must be done through the week.

But there is another kind of teaching that we are justified in doing on Sunday morning: arousing interest in the meaning of the memory work passage, helping Juniors to sense its beauty and understand the circumstances of its writing, helping them find a good motive for memorizing the passage, and recognizing the Juniors' achievements in learning the memory work.

This type of memory work teaching can be done in early time, in the class time, and in the assembly period. Perhaps the teacher's best opportunity to teach the memory work is in connection with the class time, for then both memory passage and lesson passage can be used to enrich and supplement each other.

3. *How Teach It?*

Notice that I say "use the memory work." It should be worked into the lesson, not taught as something apart. Because all the memory work is chosen for its close relation to the lessons, it is easy to relate the passage to each lesson you are teaching.

For example, the Juniors might be memorizing a passage from Psalm 119 while they are studying a unit of lessons called "Learning to Use My Bible." You see how natural it is, in the course of a lesson on Ezra's teaching God's Word, to ask the pupils to find in the psalm words that tell how Ezra felt about the Book he read from that day, or to match words in the psalm with words in the lesson, or to say a verse of the psalm as an expression of Ezra's feeling for the Book.

Or suppose your class is memorizing Romans 10:9-14 while you are teaching a lesson on the church at Antioch sending out the first foreign missionaries. You might ask the Juniors to find in the passage something the church members wanted to share with people far away; a verse that Paul might have been thinking as he sailed the blue water to Cyprus; a verse that tells what missionaries must do before pagans can believe; a verse that tells what heathen people must do; a verse that tells what we must do.

In teaching the memory work it is important that the Juniors understand the meaning of the words they memorize, and the ideas behind the words. There are adults who say, "Let the Juniors memorize now; understanding will come later." But why must they wait until later? If the teacher works at it, he can bring all words and terms of any passage suggested for Juniors to memorize, into the focus of Junior experience and understanding. (See "Use the Bible Purposefully," pp. 111-114.)

Should Juniors memorize the passages word for word,

or is it permissible for them to "learn the sense and then say it in their own words"? I might answer that question by asking whether you ever had a school teacher who permitted you to memorize a poem and say it in your own words. Of course not. Children are asked to memorize certain poems chosen for their beauty of word and thought and set down by men who were artists with words. And the beauty and artistry are lost if the original words are ignored.

Neither do we have a right to wrong a Bible passage by retelling it in our own words. It is a slipshod practice. It is doing an injustice to God's Word.

4. *The First Principle*

"You cannot teach what you do not know." That rule applies here. The first rule in guiding the learning of memory work is that the teacher memorize it himself. If a teacher does not memorize the passage, he may be teaching something about memory work he never intends to teach: "Memorizing a passage is something required of Juniors, but not of grownups." Or "When you are grown, you do not need to hide God's Word in your heart." Those are the negative lessons the Juniors are getting from your failure to memorize the passage you are teaching.

A Bible passage is not vitally learned until its truth is felt, its meaning discovered by experience. That is why it is a good idea for the teacher to use it in his devotional reading of the Bible (see chap. 2).

VI. USE VISUAL HELPS

Visual helps include pictures, maps, blackboards, objects from outdoors—any medium the teacher can use to strengthen his teaching through the use of the pupil's eyes.

1. *Pictures*

When the Junior has opportunity to see the lesson as well as hear it, when it has come to him through two senses, not just one, his total impression is strengthened. A picture breathes reality into an incident, touches it with life. Fortunately, beautiful pictures are provided with all our lessons for Juniors. And the suggestions below include ways teachers may use them to infuse life into the lessons.

(1) *A picture can explain unfamiliar Bible customs.*— How could the Shunammite family build a room for their guest "on the wall"? How could four men let down a friend through the roof of a house? How could Mary anoint the feet of Jesus while he sat at the table eating dinner?

Good pictures supply the answers to all these puzzling questions. The little room built for Elisha was built at the top of one wall of the house and extended over onto the flat roof. Roofs were made of tile which could easily be taken apart and put back. And guests sat at the table, not on chairs with their feet hidden, but reclined, oriental-fashion, on couches with their feet exposed.

Pictures help Juniors understand how people in Bible times dressed and how they lived; how the land looked and how its special quality affected their thinking and living. "Nobody in our culture can understand what a cup of cold water meant to people in Jesus' land," a friend familiar with the Holy Land said to me, "or the full meaning of a pitcher of cold water poured over hot tired feet of a traveler."

(2) *A picture can supplement the reading of the Bible passage.*—By using a picture along with the study of a Bible passage, a teacher increases the number of Bible-reading activities and enriches their possibilities.

Imagine you are teaching a lesson on Samuel helping Eli. As Juniors study a picture of Samuel and Eli in the tabernacle, they may say a Bible verse that suggests how Samuel felt about his friend, then count in the picture all the ways it suggests that Samuel helped his teacher. Or they may search the picture of Jesus healing at Peter's door to find how many diseases mentioned in the Bible passage the people in the picture seem to have. Or in the lesson on the Hebrews bringing gifts for building the tabernacle, they may match words in the passage describing what the people brought with the things shown in the picture—the bracelets, earrings, gold and purple.

(3) *A picture can introduce the reading of a Bible passage.*—Your lesson is on Timothy's family Bible, let us say. Maybe you will draw a picture frame on the board and ask the pupils to make in their minds a picture to go in the frame. You will guide them in filling in the picture by describing the lesson scene: a grandmother, a mother, a boy, and a family Bible. Then you will hold up to the frame on the board the picture showing Timothy with his family, and let pupils contrast their own mental picture with the real one. Then they will open Bibles to find the name of each and what little Timothy is discovering even as a child.

(4) *A picture can deepen appreciation of memory work.*—Let us imagine that you are teaching the lesson on the slave girl who helped Naaman, and that the memory work for the unit is Psalm 96. You might hold up the picture, then suggest that the Juniors read (or repeat) the memory passage until they come to a verse that tells what the little slave girl is doing in the picture.

Juniors may also match verses in the passage to different pictures.

(5) *A picture can bring the lesson close to everyday*

Junior living.—Some of the pictures in the lesson series show boys and girls in everyday situations. These pictures help in leading the Junior to feel that the Bible lesson has some bearing on his life today. The Juniors may compose stories built around these pictures, they may put words in the mouth of the characters in the pictures, or they may say Bible verses the characters may be saying.

2. *Maps*

Maps hold a variety of possibilities for adding interest to the lessons. Juniors may mark on a map the place where today's lesson took place; they may follow someone on a journey by tracing his footsteps on the map; they may test their recall of past lessons by putting markers on each spot where some event (called out by the teacher) took place. They may keep abreast of our present-day mission work by means of a world map.

3. *Chalkboards*

A chalkboard is really an assistant teacher. The teacher can use it to supplement his verbal teaching, to interpret unfamiliar words, to give relief from too much teacher talk, to summarize, to regain wandering attention. Sometimes a Bible verse can be illustrated by a simple drawing or diagram on the board.

VII. Get the Lesson into Living

It isn't enough for the Junior to know that it was Peter who said, "Thou art the Christ, the Son of the living God." If you were teaching a lesson on "Peter's Right Answer," your big challenge would be to help each Junior to realize that he himself must decide how he shall answer Jesus' question, "Whom do ye say that I am?" It isn't enough for the Junior to know the details of the story about Mary's love gift. He must realize that he today can bring love gifts to Jesus just as certainly as Mary did.

If the teacher has helped the Juniors know the facts of the lesson, the who, the what, the where, he has taught the lesson historically, but not personally. He has taught for a change in knowledge, but not in attitude and conduct. He has not taught a Sunday school lesson.

How can a teacher relate the lesson to Junior living? By beginning with a "you" question he may gear the lesson to the personal level (see discussion on a good beginning, pp. 109-11). Sometimes it helps to tell a story of a Junior who was faced with a situation like the one in the lesson; sometimes a series of present-day "what-would-you-do" situations based on the lesson focus attention on its here-and-now application. Always the teacher should remember the importance of the word "you."

Let us say you are teaching the lesson on Paul choosing Timothy as his missionary helper. Your purpose is to help the Juniors realize that study of God's Word while they are boys and girls helps them get ready for whatever God has for them to do. You discuss how Timothy got ready (2 Tim. 3:15) even though he did not know what work God had for him. You are getting down to real teaching when you ask, "What do you want to do when you are grown?" and lead the Juniors to realize that an understanding of the Bible helps in becoming a teacher or a doctor or a nurse (or whatever careers the pupils mention).

Sometimes it helps to personalize a verse in the passage or in the memory verse. In the lesson on "Peter's Right Answer," the teacher may get the Juniors to substitute their own names for the "ye" in Matthew 16:15: "Whom does May say that I am?" Or again, "For God so loved Jerry that he gave his only begotten Son—." Or "Jesus saith unto Sally, Go home to thy friends and tell them what great things the Lord hath done for thee." I heard a superintendent ask her Juniors the other day, "Did you

know that you are in the Bible?" Then she led them
to find in Romans 3:23 one word that means Sam and
Helen and Ruth and Peter—and all the other Juniors in
the world: "all."

Real life pictures help the Juniors to interpret the
lesson in terms of their own experiences. A picture of
a boy helping a little one who has fallen, a picture of
a girl taking a gift to a sick woman, a picture of a family going to church, or of a boy praying—all such subjects
help to translate lessons into living.

Splendid activities for getting lessons into living are
given in the pupils' quarterlies. The teacher will find
in these workbook activities many helpful ideas for applying the lesson to living. Pupils' books should be used
in class.

VIII. Give Juniors Something to Do During the Week

"Inasmuch as ye have done it unto one of the least
of these my brethren . . ." I had taught one morning, as
earnestly as I could, a lesson based on that Scripture
passage, a lesson on giving to Jesus. In the midst of our
discussion, twelve-year-old Joy exclaimed, "Please—can't
our class do something for a poor family? We never
have."

I felt that morning that I had prepared a good lesson,
but Joy's question made me realize that I had failed in
a most important point. I had planned to arouse my
pupils' desire to help those in need, but I had not come
prepared with any definite suggestion for putting that
desire into action. The incident taught me a lesson. I
always try to see my lesson in terms of deeds that
Carol and Elaine and Sandra and Lydia can do *this
week*.

If the teacher has taught a lesson on being strong in
times of temptation, his carry-over activity might be to
have the Christian pupils learn the memory verse, "I

can do all things through Christ which strengtheneth me," and repeat it every morning as a reminder to turn to Jesus for help in temptation. If the lesson has sought to lead Juniors to be great in Jesus' way, the teacher might suggest that Juniors have a "hidden-greatness search," watching for people who show greatness in Jesus' way. Or the teacher, out of his own knowledge of each Junior's home background, might prepare a list of home duties for every pupil in a lesson on "helping in my home," and let the pupils write the day of the week by every job they perform on that day.

These are just suggestions. For every lesson there is a possibility of a carry-over activity. The teacher should always think of the lesson in terms of something to do during the week. Since Junior memories are short, it is a good idea to give the Juniors some sort of reminder, perhaps a self-check sheet or a memorandum of the assignment to keep in their Bibles.

LET'S THINK

1. Where should a Junior go directly on arrival at Sunday school?

2. Mention three activities appropriate to the early time.

3. What is the main disadvantage in beginning a lesson by having pupils "read from their Bibles"?

4. Give one reason why it is advisable to:
   Give the Juniors something to look for as they use Bibles in class
   Put Bible reading early in lesson
   Be sure that Juniors understand unfamiliar words and ideas

5. What is the difference between *reading* the Bible and *using* the Bible in Sunday school?

6. If you were teaching a lesson on being brave in times of danger, and you wanted to suggest a carry-over activity for the coming week, what definite thing would you ask the Juniors to do?

BEYOND SUNDAY MORNING

The teacher learns most about his pupils by studying them in natural, everyday situations, by watching (and sharing in) their play—by listening to (and sharing in) their talk as they meet in informal groups.

I. VISITS IN THE HOME
    1. Visit to Round Out Your Picture of the Pupil
    2. Visit to Get Necessary Record Information
    3. Visit to Help Juniors Improve in Their Sunday School Work
    4. Visit to Represent Your Church
    5. Visit to Win to Christ
    6. Visit to Be a Friend

II. CLASS MEETINGS
    1. The Need for Knowing the Whole Pupil
    2. Procedure for a Class Meeting
    3. Other Weekday Opportunities
    4. The Value of Weekday Meetings Summarized

III. MAIL CONTACTS
    1. To Commend Good Work
    2. To Serve as Special Reminders
    3. To Honor Certain Occasions

IV. PARENT-WORKER MEETINGS
    1. Who Attends?
    2. Where Meeting Is Held
    3. How to Proceed

V. WEEKLY WORKERS' MEETING
    1. What the Teacher Gets
    2. What the Teacher Gives

CHAPTER IX

BEYOND SUNDAY MORNING

Sunday morning is over, your lesson period is past, and you face what many regard as the teacher's most serious handicap: six days before another class-time opportunity, six days in which Juniors can unlearn, forget assignments, grow indifferent to a project, lose the sense of oneness and togetherness so necessary to a fine class spirit.

The weekday stretch between Sundays *is* a handicap—but there are teachers who find ways to overcome it, who know how to translate that handicap into opportunity. They cannot reduce the number of days between Sundays, but they *can* reduce the number of days between contacts with their pupils. They have learned that it is not necessary to shut up shop when they shut the classroom door on Sunday morning; that Monday, Tuesday, Wednesday, and the other weekdays offer almost as many opportunities for doing Sunday school business as Sunday morning.

The only teacher really blocked by six days between Sundays is the "Sunday morning teacher," the one whose vision of his opportunities never goes beyond the four walls of the classroom or over the boundary set by his forty-minute allotment for teaching.

This chapter will be concerned with ways teachers may get over those walls, may step over that boundary.

I. VISITS IN THE HOME

I have noticed one similarity among most of the teachers who complain that there is one pupil or more whom they "simply can't do anything with." Usually those teachers answer no to one important question, the question that must be asked in getting at the roots of the problem: Have you been in that pupil's home?

Why should a Sunday school teacher visit? Because he teaches! "You cannot teach whom you do not know," and you cannot know any pupil until you know the influences that have helped make him what he is. The best place to study these influences is in the home.

The path to better Junior work leads down the path to a Junior's front door.

The teacher visits for a purpose.

A visit, like a Sunday school lesson, will be purposeful only if the teacher knows what he wants to do and goes into the home to do it. The home is so important to the teacher's work that he should always use the visits to achieve something positive, something that will strengthen his teaching and bring home and Sunday school nearer together in their purposes. For example:

1. *Visit to Round Out Your Picture of the Pupil*

Everything that pertains to the quality of living in this home is important to the teacher. It is not necessary to ask point-blank questions to find out the essentials; so much can be sensed: the level of Christian standards, whether or not the parents attend church, have family worship, are sympathetic with the purposes of the Sunday school. Sometimes in a talk with parents, confidential information comes out—information that deepens the teacher's insight into the pupils' problems.

I heard once of an eleven-year-old girl who dropped out of Sunday school for no apparent reason. On talking with the parents, the teacher learned that this pupil had only a second-grade reading ability and that the teacher's practice of having the pupils read in turn from the Bible made her feel so inferior that she stayed home rather than undergo the shame and humiliation that experience caused her.

Valuable information about the Junior's interests will usually come out in the course of conversation—information about his hobbies, his interests, his activities, and his relationship with the other members of the family. All such facts, stored away in the teacher's mind, will be of help in guiding the Junior personally, in applying teaching to that pupil's individual situations. Larry's elderly grandmother, Mark's baby brother, Tony's invalid father, should suggest ways to translate future Sunday school lessons into living.

2. *Visit to Get Necessary Record Information*

The information given the teacher about his pupils is often inaccurate, and more often incomplete. One of the teacher's purposes, on the first visit at least, is to right his facts about each pupil, get home address, telephone number, birthday, church affiliation of parents, number of people in the family.

3. *Visit to Help Juniors Improve in Their Sunday School Work*

Why do so many Juniors attend Sunday school irregularly? Come in late on Sunday morning? Fail to learn the memory work? Go home after Sunday school? Isn't it because usually there is no one in the home following up the teacher's efforts, giving weekday encouragement in these important areas, nudging memories? In their visits teachers have a wonderful opportunity to talk with parents about such problems.

(1) *Stress the necessity of regular attendance at Sunday school.*—No matter how carefully the teacher plans for Sunday morning, those plans are wasted if the pupils are not there, and weakened if the pupils attend spasmodically.

Many times it helps lay this responsibility on the parents' hearts if the teacher explains that the Sunday school lessons are written in units, and that an absentee misses more than one lesson; he misses one segment of a carefully planned whole, one step in a big purpose. Parents also should face the fact that missing one Sunday from Sunday school compares with missing more than a week of day school.

(2) *Enlist parents' co-operation in getting their Junior to arrive on time—preferably ahead of time.*—Acquaint the parents with the early time program. Some parents will need to be told the hour at which Sunday school begins; I have talked with mothers who, though their children had attended Sunday school for years, were still vague about the exact hour at which Sunday school started.

(3) *Explain the requirements of a studied lesson.*—(The Junior must read the lesson in the quarterly and in the Bible, learn a memory verse, and do a reasonable amount of any suggested written work.)

(4) *Acquaint parents with the reason for Juniors' bringing the Bible—a whole Bible, not just a Testament—to Sunday school.*—All parents need to understand that in the Junior years their child, for the first time in his Sunday school experience, is using his Bible in the class period; that his Sunday school lesson is now based on discussion and Scripture searching rather than on the telling of a Bible story.

Parents should understand that a pupil without a Bible is crippled in the study of the lesson and the pupil with a New Testament only is usually left out at some time during lesson or assembly.

(5) *Enlist parents' interest and co-operation in the learning of the memory work.*—It will be necessary to explain to some parents what you mean by the term, and

where it is listed in the pupil's book, and the time by which each passage should be learned. One of the most valuable uses of the visit is to discuss with parents the benefit of the memory work to the child's mind and spirit now and throughout his life.

(6) *Discuss another all-important "major" in Junior Sunday school work: the fact that Junior years are the churchgoing years.*—It is a matter of interest to parents that until Junior years a child is not required to attend the preaching service in order to be a 100 per cent pupil.

The aid of parents should be enlisted in the higher reaches of our church-attendance purposes, in the fact that in Junior years we seek to help Juniors form the habit of participation in the church services, in concentrating on the sermon for the help it will give them later. To both parents and teachers it is a fact for serious consideration that Juniors may be forming the habit of non-attention while they are forming the habit of attending church; that puts on both the responsibility for enriching the sermon for the Junior, discussing it with him, motivating his listening.

The preceding suggestions do not claim to be a complete list of topics for discussion with parents in the homes. They merely suggest some general guideposts for making visits more purposeful. It may be that other topics of equal importance should be discussed from time to time.

4. *Visit to Represent Your Church*

A teacher visiting in a home is more than a Sunday school teacher visiting a pupil. He is *his church* out working among people. As its representative, he should be informed about its various services and organizations, ready to suggest ways it can minister to every age and every spiritual need. The teacher may feel himself a very insignificant part of the church, but to this family, perhaps new in town, he *is* that church. In their eyes, his spirit and attitude reflect that of the entire membership and often determine whether the family decide to unite their lives with his church or another.

The teacher will be alert for all information of interest to church and pastor. He should know enough about the Sunday school to say a word about the classes to which various members should go and about the teachers of those classes. The family needs to know about the various facilities of the church that affect each member—the Nursery, the Extension department, library, Music Ministry, all Junior organizations.

Information of interest to the pastor should be turned over to him and names of prospective members handed to the proper classes and departments.

5. *Visit to Win to Christ*

Often as he visits, the teacher finds that one parent, or both, are not Christians. When that is the case he will, of course, with God's help, seek to win them to Christ. Some teachers find that an appropriate leaflet or a Gospel of John with certain verses marked help to reinforce their own words. The pastor's help should always be enlisted and the help of teachers of Adult classes.

It helps, too, if the teacher shares the names of unsaved parents with the teachers in the Junior group and asks their prayers. Some superintendents prepare, for the teachers to use in their devotions, prayer lists containing the names of parents—and Juniors, too—who are not Christians.

Certainly the teacher will need to go back to visit the parent who is unsaved. He will always seek prayerfully to say the right words and will not be discouraged if his efforts are not immediately rewarded. Above all he will let those mothers and fathers feel that he is motivated by love and concern for them. That is the most compelling force in the world. The teacher should remember that he has an advantage in this soul-winning enterprise. He shares with the parents an interest in the object of their dearest concern. That gives him a point of contact, and entrance to their attention and hearts, an authority and a right to speak not shared, perhaps, by any other person, not even their pastor. It is one of the teacher's most sacred trusts.

So often the teacher finds it necessary to visit the parents in order to talk about the matter of their child becoming a Christian. Sometimes both parents and teacher share a concern in the fact that the Junior has not become a Christian; more often the teacher visits because he feels convinced that the Junior is a Christian and the parent objects to his making a profession of faith. What can the teacher do in this latter case? He may pray with the parent; he may suggest that the parent let the preacher talk with his child to determine whether or not he has really had an experience of Christ. Best of all, he may suggest to the Junior that he try to live each day before his mother and father in such a way that they will not question the fact of his conversion.

6. Visit to Be a Friend

That purpose should underlie every visit. Unless he is accepted as a friend by both parents and their Junior, the teacher will never realize the highest reaches of his usefulness. In every visit he should interest himself in the parents' interests; make their concerns his concerns, look for ways to express his friendship.

But when I say "visit to be a friend," I am thinking now of a special kind of visit. It is not the visit called for by any schedule or a program, not a visit made because the pupil is new and should be visited within the week; not the visit made because a pupil has been absent two or three Sundays, or is sick or bereaved. All these circumstances demand a visit and should find the teacher in the home with pupil and parents; certainly the conscientious teacher will visit at these times. But these visits are in the line of duty, and I am thinking of one that goes beyond the call of duty, the visit motivated by simple friendship, by genuine liking and the human pleasure of sharing; the visit where the teacher drops by to say, "Happy birthday," or "Here is a stamp for your collection," or "Here is the new quarterly," or "I was interested to see whether you have learned the rest of your memory passage," or "I think you might like this book," or "I wanted to be here when Mother came back from the hospital."

The teacher whose relationship to his pupils is friend to friend as well as teacher to pupil has laid a sound foundation for an effective teaching ministry.

II. CLASS MEETINGS

1. *The Need for Knowing the Whole Pupil*

Throughout this book I have tried to stress one teaching imperative: the absolute necessity for a teacher to know his pupils if he is to help them in their living. He needs to know the *whole* pupil, how he plays and works and reacts to other boys and girls. The teacher can learn some things by listening to his pupils on Sunday morning. He can learn more by studying the pupil in his home. But he learns most of all by observing those he teaches in natural, everyday situations, by watching (and sharing in) their play, by listening to (and joining in) their talk as they meet together on weekdays.

That is the most important reason for weekday meetings of teacher and pupils. A teacher told me that he could learn more by watching his pupils in one afternoon's ball game than in many months of Sunday mornings.

That is one reason for the emphasis on regular class meetings for Juniors and their teacher. There should be such a meeting at least once a month. These meetings may be held in the home of the teacher, in the home of a pupil, or at the church. If for any reason, these locations are not practical, then the teacher must use his imagination to find some other place of meeting. One teacher I know meets her girls after school at a drugstore near the school at their regular meeting time and there, at a table in the back reserved for them, guides the meeting and enjoys talk and refreshments with them. Another has solved the problem by having the girls meet her for supper once a month at the regular church supper in the social hall. They sit together at a table reserved for them and have their meeting and discuss their class plans.

Sometimes a boys' class will form a ball team and meet regularly with the teacher for a game. This provides all of them with an opportunity to enjoy a game, one another, and to strengthen their feeling for the class. *The class that plays together stays together.*

2. Procedure for a Class Meeting

The class meeting, no matter what its activities, should include a brief business session, a look at records, a discussion of special emphases, and the carrying out of any activities related to lessons, memory work, or units that are more appropriate to weekdays than Sunday morning.

There is usually a social period following the business meeting, a time for playing a game or two and refreshments.

Sometimes, instead of games, the teacher may guide in some interesting memory work activity, such as the illustrating of a Bible passage, or the making of booklets or posters. Or some time may be devoted to a project relating to the lessons, such as packing a box for a missionary or a mission Sunday school or making friendship cards (using verses from memory work) for the pastor or other friends.

3. *Other Weekday Opportunities*

The class meeting is not the only opportunity afforded the teacher for happy weekday contacts with his pupils. Often trips to places of interest in the community give opportunity to extend some phase of the lesson into the week. This might take the form of a trip to a Jewish synagogue, a trip to the children's home, the home for the aged, or to a mission Sunday school.

4. *The Value of Weekday Meetings Summarized*

Besides the big value stressed previously—that of helping the teacher get a better insight into the nature of his pupils—the weekday meetings have other values. They help to promote class spirit and develop initiative and leadership on the part of class members. And finally—and this might be as important as any other value—the meeting gives teacher and pupils a chance to have a happy time together, to enjoy each other's company. Through the class meeting the teacher says vividly to the pupils: "Religion is not something reserved for Sunday morning. It is for all days, something to live by, play by, choose by."

III. Mail Contacts

While letters and cards never substitute for person-to-person contacts, they do supplement them and strengthen the relationship between pupils and teacher. Through letters the teacher may get into the homes of all his pupils any day in any week. He may go back again and again, thus multiplying his efforts indefinitely. Because letters are still a novelty to Juniors, they have an importance in their eyes that is lost on older people.

Some ways in which a teacher may use letters and cards are:

1. *To Commend Good Work*

Good work is its own reward, of course, and the teacher should try always to help his pupils realize that. But we all know that a word of encouragement, spoken or written, not only helps a pupil's morale, but often spurs his will to improve. A letter that does that is well worth an investment of the postage and a few minutes of time.

A marked improvement in preaching attendance or in memorizing Bible passages or in punctual arrival merit a written note from the teacher. They serve still another purpose: They often arouse the parents' interest in this phase of work and give them an impetus to offer home encouragement.

Of course this practice, if overdone, will defeat its own purpose. Commendations depreciate in value if they are too frequent. Wait until the pupil does something that really deserves praise, then write a note to say, "I noticed; I am proud of you."

2. *To Serve as Special Reminders*

Because there are six days between Sundays and because Juniors have short memories, it is often necessary to give a weekday reminder of some assignment or some activity. A written one is better than a telephoned reminder because it has *staying* value. Then, too, written reminders sometimes nudge a Junior's will to improve his work. If Sharon is shaky in her preaching attendance, the teacher can send a little note on Friday to bolster up her resolve (or her mother's) to attend Sunday. If Nancy and Sarah have almost memorized 1 Corinthians 13, a brief letter sent during the week may encourage complete memorization by Sunday. If Vera is chronically late, a note hinting at some good activity to be enjoyed next Sunday in early time might get the desired result.

3. *To Honor Certain Occasions*

There are certain occasions in a Junior's life that should receive special recognition by his teacher. A letter serves to magnify the occasion and to warm the hearts of both Juniors and parents.

When a Junior joins the church, the teacher should write him a letter expressing his happiness over his decision to be a Christian, and his hope that he will grow as a good follower of Jesus. Such a letter may be treasured for a lifetime by both Junior and parents.

Many teachers write letters of welcome to new pupils as well as letters to those who are leaving. It is an especially nice thing for teachers of twelve-year-olds to write letters to their pupils as they enter the Intermediate department. If the Junior goes away for the summer, the teacher should keep in touch with him by mail.

IV. PARENT-WORKER MEETINGS

Training boys and girls in full-time Christian living is a full-time Christian job. It calls for positive effort seven days a week, fifty-two weeks a year. It requires a togetherness of thinking and proceeding on the part of those most actively at work on the job: parents and Sunday school teachers.

In addition to the two methods already discussed for getting parents and teachers together in their work (visits and letters) there is a third: meetings of workers and parents.

1. *Who Attends?*

Such a meeting is attended, of course, by teachers and officers of the Junior group and by Junior parents.

If the workers want to get yet another value from the meeting, they will include the Juniors. This gives Juniors opportunity to enjoy a good time together as members of the Sunday school and as members of their families. It also insures better parent attendance.

2. Where Meeting Is Held

If space is available, it is better to have the parent meeting at the church. Special provision should be made for entertaining the Juniors in a room apart from that in which teachers and parents meet. The two groups come together later for a social hour.

The program for Juniors should be supervised by some competent person or persons from outside the Junior department. (All Junior workers are needed in the meeting with parents.) Entertainment may include songs, stunts, games, quizzes, stories, a good film, or the tricks of a magician.

The best place of meeting for the parents is in the Junior rooms. There is value in having them sit where their children sit on Sunday, view the same surroundings, get a firsthand look at the department's equipment (or observe the lack of it) and perhaps see some of the work their children are doing.

3. How to Proceed

Now what is the best use of the time when parents and teachers come together for the meeting? The answer is obvious: Use it to decide how you can best work together for the good of the Juniors.

The first step is to face, before the meeting, the problems on which you need the parents' help. These might include too-few conversions, failure of Juniors to attend preaching services, indifference to memory work, lack of home study, lack of parent interest in the whole Sunday school program.

Next ask, "How can we get these problems out before the parents in the most interesting and forceful way?" One answer is by the use of mimeographed sheets listing the questions you have slated for discussion. You can strengthen this discussion by the use of panel, that is, several people especially equipped to contribute to the questions, carefully chosen people who will be able to throw out a thought or summarize a conclusion.

Here is a way you might phrase some questions to bring the above named problems into focus: When is a child ready to join the church? Is regular preaching attendance necessary to a Junior's best development? On how many points are Juniors marked each Sunday? Which of these points are required of Juniors—and not of younger children? When does your child study his Sunday school lesson? How can teachers make the lesson more applicable to your child's life? Why are Juniors given more memory work to learn than any other group in the Sunday school? How can parents encourage Juniors to attend and participate in the church service each Sunday?

There are other possibilities for getting a home-church problem into the spotlight. It might be done through a film or a talk made by some competent person. But whatever method is used, there should always be opportunity for free discussion. That is the best way to get your group to thinking, to keep them interested. It is the way to bring problems and questions out in the open, to let the teachers get a glimpse into the parents' thinking.

Whatever opinions the parents express, those opinions should be respected. The teachers' attitude should never be, "We have brought you here to tell you something you should know," but, "Here is a problem in which we are both interested. Let's consider how we can work together to solve it in the light of what is best for your child."

V. WEEKLY WORKERS' MEETING

A detailed treatment of this subject belongs more properly in a book devoted to Junior Sunday school administration. However, since our purpose in this chapter is to examine all the opportunities weekdays offer teachers for improving their work, we cannot overlook such a rich one as the workers' meeting. The chance to come together each week with his fellow teachers for studying and planning is one of the finest advantages a church can offer a teacher.

1. *What the Teacher Gets*

The reason for the meeting's value is suggested by one little word in that last sentence: "together." Group thinking is bound to be more fruitful than private thinking. It is a case where the sum of a thing is greater than its parts. There is something about the coming together of minds that sparks ideas from other minds, that stimulates all to better thinking.

The teacher who says, "But I don't have the time" is minute-wise and hour-foolish. Studying together in the weekly meeting *saves* time. One hour's study together yields a richer harvest than two hours' study alone.

The weekly meeting keeps the teacher reminded to study early in the week, with the result that he has a longer time to meditate on the lesson, to let it sink down into his experience and flow into the bloodstream of his thinking and feeling.

The advantage of the apprentice principle applies in the weekly meeting. This is a workshop in which the new, inexperienced teacher labors alongside the experienced one, benefiting from his experience, drawing on his wisdom, gaining from his superior skill.

In this meeting the teacher becomes the beneficiary of the accumulated experiences of a whole group of people through the years. Methods that have failed and those that have succeeded, ideas for reading the Bible and for applying lessons to life, all provide a backlog of helps that may later on help a teacher transfuse life into many a Sunday school lesson.

There is another advantage in the weekly meeting. Just listening to the experiences of others, knowing that they have the same problems and discouragements, the same obstacles and failures, helps a teacher right his perspective, recover morale.

2. What the Teacher Gives

The teacher has some responsibilities, too, toward a meeting that offers him so much. He should have a conscience about his obligation to attend with as much regularity as possible. It is an opportunity to be an example, to witness, to contribute to something his Sunday school considers important.

A teacher has a responsibility to study his lesson before he comes to the meeting. Quite obviously he cannot contribute helpfully unless he has studied. Without previous study he cannot even *get* much help. Unless he has put his own mind to work on the passage under discussion, he has no foundation on which to work with the other teachers to build a lesson.

So a Sunday school teacher cannot be just a *Sunday* teacher. If he is worthy of the name, he will be a Monday teacher, a Thursday teacher, a *weekday* teacher. He will refuse to be walled in by the four walls of his classroom and restricted by the forty-minute limit set on his teaching time.

His classroom is as wide as his town—and his teaching opportunities include all the hours of all the weeks.

LET'S THINK

1. If someone said to you, "A teacher can learn all he needs to know about his pupils by keeping his eyes and ears open on Sunday morning," would you agree? If you disagree, tell why.

2. Make a list of several weekday opportunities the teacher has for contacts with his pupils. Which do you think are the most valuable?

3. Name three opportunities to enlist the interest of parents available to any teacher.

4. In a parent-worker meeting, why do you think an open discussion with parents and teachers participating is more valuable than a formal talk or an address?

5. Name two ways in which the weekly workers' meeting benefits the inexperienced teacher. Name one way in which experienced teachers may help new ones in this meeting.

SUGGESTIONS FOR THE TEACHER

WHO WILL GUIDE IN THE STUDY OF THIS BOOK

Prior to the first class period, learn all you can about the prospective members of your study class. Will they all be from your church? from one department? from several churches? What Junior lesson courses will be used in the various departments which will be represented in your class? (One or more years of closely Graded lessons; or the lessons for all ages of Juniors; or perhaps all of these.)

What can you learn about the quality of teaching being done in the departments which will be represented in your class? How effectively does the superintendent lead the teaching improvement activities in the weekly officers and teachers' meetings?

Perhaps many of these questions cannot be answered before the class begins. Certainly, you will need to be alert throughout the class periods and in personal conferences for any insights which you can gain as to specific needs in your group.

PURPOSE

After you have studied the textbook and considered all you can learn about the prospective members of your study class, write out your own statement of what you hope will be accomplished by means of this study. State your purpose in terms of changes in knowledge, in attitudes, in conduct and skills.

SCHEDULE

Determine where the greatest emphasis is needed in line with the needs of your class members. In particular, note chapter 7 and the suggestions for teaching it. You may wish to assign the suggested activities for that chapter at the first period of the study class, in order to give members time to work on the preparation of the Sunday school lesson and the plan sheet, as assigned. In order to allow extra time for chapter 7, perhaps you will need to move rapidly through some of the preceding chapters, selecting only a few of the suggested learning activities for use with your class.

PROCEDURES

Probably, for each chapter of the book, you will lead class members to observe the picture at the beginning and to consider the implications in the statement under the picture. Class members may use the chapter outline on the chalkboard or a flipchart as a guide in recalling their previous study of the textbook material. They should be led to discuss the implications of the statements and topics in the outlines. The suggestions under "Let's Think" at the close of each chapter should stimulate class discussion.

You will wish to introduce other learning activities as additions or alternates to the foregoing. The following are merely suggested:

Chapter 1

Ask class members to find and read the author's statement of purpose on page 3. Raise the question: To what extent may we expect to "find in the example of Jesus as a Junior some suggestions for guiding our own Juniors, some purposes to work toward in our teaching"? Lead your class to discover and state five things that were true of Jesus as a Junior and that we seek to make true of our Juniors (see pp. 4-6).

Lead your class to examine the quotation by Dr. Mullins on page 12 to discover terms which he suggests for use with Juniors. Let members list some doctrinal phrases and theological terms often used with adults but unsuited for Juniors, and then suggest alternate terms which would be more meaningful for a Junior.

Chapter 2

Using the chapter outline, have the class read together ten statements about a teacher's qualifications (five under I and five more listed as headings II-VI). For silent self-examination, ask: Which of these qualities do you possess, at least in some degree? In which are you particularly seeking to grow? What are you doing to help yourself grow in these characteristics? Then ask members to share suggestions about how a group of Junior workers can help one another to grow in these characteristics.

Chapter 3

Call attention to the five headings under which Junior purposes are grouped on pages 40-41. Divide the class into five groups (more if subdivision according to the various units of lessons being taught seems wise). Let each group use a buzz session to examine the current quarter's lessons for the purpose of analyzing the stated teaching purposes. The first group may look for purposes that relate to the Bible; the next for those that relate to the church; and so on. After a stated number of minutes, let each group report its findings. Help class members to see that while some one of these areas of purpose usually dominates, many other areas will also be strengthened in a given unit.

If possible, give each member of your class the full statement of "The Objectives of Christian Teaching and Training" for Juniors. Lead workers to compare this fuller list with the summary of teaching purposes given on pages 40-42 of this textbook.

Chapter   4

Divide your class into three groups. Make previous assignments to the first group to find, in lessons in the current unit, illustrations of ideas for securing readiness on the part of the pupils. Let the second group find illustrations of use of the law of satisfaction, and the third group find illustrations of the law of exercise. Each group will be ready to cite illustrations during the class period.

(Note: As teacher, you should be ready to supplement the reports of these groups with specific illustrations from a current unit.)

Chapter 5

Group class members according to the kinds of lessons being studied. Instruct each group: Consider the last unit of lessons used with your Juniors. List some specific changes in the pupils which you feel sure came about as a result of that unit of study. Tell how you can discern such changes.

After the group reports, ask the class to compile a list of

tasks a teacher might set for himself in order to prepare himself to be a more effective teacher.

Chapter 6

Again divide your class into groups according to the unit of lessons being taught. Ask each group to examine the current unit (or the next unit, if a new unit will soon be started) in order to discover—

1. How many lessons it includes.
2. Why this group of lessons constitutes a unit.
3. The unit purpose.

Ask each group to examine as many lessons in the unit as time permits, seeking to discover how each lesson should change pupils. The group should decide whether the lesson aims mainly at changes in knowledge, attitudes, or conduct. (Most lessons will major on only one of these areas.) After a brief buzz session, let each group report its findings.

Chapter 7

Lead class members to compare the guide sheet for a lesson plan as given on page 101 with other guide sheets found in their teacher's Sunday school lesson books, *Nine- and Ten-Year Junior Superintendent's Manual, Book One* (p. 55), or in free literature on Junior work. Select the guide sheet which seems to you most helpful and use it as a guide in the following activities.

Ask the class to follow the steps in the outline on page 88 as they study next Sunday's lesson. Urge them to do as much as possible of this study before the class period. For the most effective preparation, they should begin this study as early in the week as possible. During the class period lead your members to use a lesson plan sheet as a guide in writing their teaching plans for the following Sunday. If various members of your class will be teaching different lessons, divide into groups according to the lessons being taught. Ask members of each group to exchange ideas on the points in the plan sheet. During this group discussion each class member should complete and revise his plan sheet as needed.

When all the groups come together again, have them exchange statements of what has been discovered about how to improve their skills in lesson planning.

Lead the group to decide if there is some particular step at which added help is needed. For example, class members may request help in how to use the source books listed under IV of the outline. If necessary, they should plan to use part of another period for helping one another at the points of greatest need.

Chapter 8

Using the outline on page 104, lead your class members to test the plans which they have prepared, as directed in connection with chapter 7. Use such questions as the following:

1. What interesting activities have you planned for Juniors as they arrive?
2. How will you make the transition from these activities to what may be called "the lesson itself"? (Of course all of the activities are part of your teaching and will relate to your lesson purpose.)
3. Do your plans for purposeful Bible using include all the factors listed under III?
4. Have you planned to use memory verses and memory work as correlated parts of your lesson development?
5. What visual helps will you use? Do you have them ready and in good condition?
6. How will you get the lesson "into Junior living"?
7. What will you ask your Juniors to do about this lesson during the week?

Chapter 9

Ask each class member to use the suggestions in this chapter as a guide, and to draw up for himself a list of things he plans to do for each Junior in his class, in order to be a seven-days-a-week teacher. Suggest that each one schedule a target date for each item in his list, by which time he hopes to complete it.

SOME SUGGESTED VISUAL MATERIALS

The filmstrip *Junior Sunday School Work* (40 frames with manual) highlights many of the principles of teaching discussed in these pages. It could be used effectively to introduce or to conclude the course.

The "Teacher Improvement Series" is a set of five filmstrips each of which concerns one aspect of teaching: *The Christian Teacher* (44 frames), *Selecting Aims* (38 frames), *Choosing Methods* (40 frames), *Planning a Lesson* (33 frames), *Testing Results* (33 frames). Selected frames will enrich the teaching of chapters 2, 6, 7, and 8. For descriptions and prices consult your current *Baptist Book Store Catalog*.

The filmstrip entitled *The Preadolescent,* which shows many characteristics of Junior boys and girls, would be excellent to use when discussing chapter 3, "These Are Your Juniors."

BIBLIOGRAPHY

DOBBINS, GAINES S. *Winning the Children* (1953)

EDGE, FINDLEY B. *Helping the Teacher* (1959)

FORD, LEROY. *A Primer for Teachers and Leaders* (1963)

———. *Tools for Teaching and Training* (1961)

GESELL, ARNOLD, and ILG, FRANCES L. *Child from Five to Ten* (1946)

GESELL, ARNOLD, *et al. Youth: The Years from Ten to Sixteen* (1956)

HERON, FRANCES D. *Jay Bain, Junior Boy* (1963)

HOWSE, WILLIAM LEWIS. *Those Treasured Hours* (1960)

WALDRUP, EARL. *Teaching and Training with Audio-Visuals* (1962)

FOR REVIEW AND WRITTEN WORK

Chapter 1

1. From a study of Jesus' experiences in the Temple when he was twelve years old (Luke 2:41–52), list five facts that we know about Jesus as a Junior.
2. How many of these statements about Jesus suggest purposes we would like to see realized in the lives of our juniors?
3. Name at least one good reason for seeking to lead Juniors to Jesus while they are Juniors.
4. What responsibility does a teacher have after he has won a Junior to Christ?

Chapter 2

5. Name four fundamental things in which a good teacher of Juniors will believe.
6. List at least two things that a co-operative teacher will do.
7. List some questions that a teacher might ask himself if he feels that he is "too old to teach."

Chapter 3

8. What are some ways in which Juniors differ from younger children physically? Mentally?
9. State briefly one attainable purpose for Juniors: in relation to the Bible; in relation to the church; in relation to Jesus.

Chapter 4

10. What are some factors that condition a Junior's readiness to learn?
11. Why are prizes and other material rewards poor motives for learning in Sunday school?

Chapter 5

12. What three types of lesson preparation should a teacher make?
13. List some opportunities a teacher has to study his pupils.

Chapter 6

14. How early should a teacher begin studying next Sunday's lesson?

15. Should a teacher always adopt the lesson writer's purposes just as they are?
16. What does a teacher know about his class that no lesson writer can possibly know?

Chapter 7

17. Why should a teacher read the Bible passage devotionally before he teaches his lesson?
18. List three advantages in writing down a lesson plan.

Chapter 8

19. Why should a Junior go directly to his teacher on arrival at Sunday school?
20. List some ways a teacher may "get the lesson into living."
21. Why should Bible reading in a Junior class be different from Bible reading in an Adult class?

Chapter 9

22. Name at least three weekday responsibilities of a Sunday school teacher.
23. List some purposes of a visit into a Junior's home.
24. What are some values a teacher gets from studying with other workers in the weekly meeting?